FOR THE LOVE OF
MOOKIE, MIKE, AND
DAVID WRIGHT

ALAN ROSS

CUMBERLAND HOUSE
NASHVILLE, TENNESSEE

METS PRIDE
CUMBERLAND HOUSE PUBLISHING, INC.
An imprint of Turner Publishing Company
Nashville, Tennessee
www.turnerpublishing.com

Cover design: Gore Studio, Inc., Nashville, Tennessee
Book design: John Mitchell

Content was compiled from a variety of sources and appears as originally presented; thus, some factual errors and differences in accounts may exist.

Library of Congress Cataloging-in-Publication Data

Ross, Alan, 1944-
  Mets pride : for the love of Mookie, Mike, and David Wright / Alan Ross.
     p. cm.
  Includes bibliographical references and index.
  ISBN-13: 978-1-58182-578-7 (pbk. : alk. paper)
  ISBN-10: 1-58182-578-1 (pbk. : alk. paper)
  1. New York Mets (Baseball team)—History. 2. New York Mets (Baseball team)—History—Quotations, maxims, etc. I. Title.

  GV875.N38R67 2007
  796.35709747′1—dc22

                                              2006101716

Printed in the United States of America

1 2 3 4 5 6 7—13 12 11 10 09 08

For John Glennon,
an Arizona Amazin'
and
for Caroline,
my dearest love

Ron Swoboda

CONTENTS

FOREWORD

It was April 1963, and my Fordham University roommate and I had tired of New York City's unrelenting grey, dank winters. In a toast to the newfound warmth of approaching springtime, The Beast suggested that we transport ourselves out the door and head for the Polo Grounds.

"Let's check out the Mets," he said, in what was a thinly veiled excuse to go see his beloved Cubbies, visiting from Chicago, his hometown. Like chirping baby robins, we lighted onto the "el" that sped us quickly from our Bronx tenement apartment down to 155th Street off the Harlem River, site of one of sport's hallowed venues, where McGraw's venerable Giants championship teams of an earlier time held sway and present home to Casey Stengel's barely manageable New York Mets.

We were both apprised of the fact that the Mets were high comedy, a mirthful cherry bomb somehow tossed into professional sports' kingdom of austere reverence. It was with that foreknowledge that we felt privileged that afternoon, staring directly into the sun from our bleacher seats aside the center-field clubhouse, to witness one of an endless line of legendary Mets mishaps.

While first baseman "Marvelous" Marv Throne-berry hogged most of the spotlight for the Mets' dumbfounding parade of blunders, it was Frank Thomas, a former three-time All-Star with the Pirates, playing center field on this occasion, who wrested the mantle of dubious infamy from Throneberry. The Beast and I chortled as Thomas moved in on a simple base hit to center, only to have the ball bound through his legs a la Bill Buckner, who 23 years later would carve his own indelible place into Mets history. The ball rolled all the way back to Grant's monument, 500 feet from home plate.

The winner that long-ago April day, the score, and any other game-related matters are lost to memory. Only the glow of Thomas's fielding gaffe remains, much treasured in the mind's archives.

Lo these many years later, *Mets Pride* is birthed, imparting the story of New York Mets baseball, as told by the players, managers, coaches, opponents, fans, and the media. It salutes the great stars, teams, moments, rivalries, fans, and origins of the Amazin's, including chapters on the Mets' all-time team and the world championship rosters.

From Marv to Mookie, Backman to Beltran, Hernandez to HoJo, Piazza to Pedro, and Knight to Wright, it's all Mets.

REMEMBRANCE

Six years following my glorious introduction to New York Mets baseball (see Foreword), I was out of school and into my second job in New York City, a glam gig envied by many in my age bracket—that of a production coordinator for the National Broadcasting Company's flagship owned and operated station, WNBC-TV. My typical work schedule found me assisting on such local fare as *Research Project*, hosted by weatherman Dr. Frank Field, and *New York Illustrated*, an award-winning broadcast news/documentary magazine. But one special day in late March of 1969, an assignment to be remembered came in.

I was to head for Shea Stadium and videotape five public service announcements with Mets players and/or coaches. I excitedly wrote out my "wish" list: Tommie Agee, Cleon Jones, Ron Swoboda, Yogi Berra (then a coach) and manager Gil Hodges. The day of the taping dawned cold and drizzly. The camera crew and I were shown onto a soggy field just as batting practice began and were told by some public relations assistant that we were on our own for getting whom we wanted for the PSAs, if the players themselves were willing.

Hmmm . . . okay, then. "Ahem, excuse me Tommie, I'm with WNBC-TV. . . . " "Hello, Yogi, do you have a minute?" "Hey, Cleon! We're doing some public service—" et cetera. Much to the credit of those Mets mentioned, all were graciously willing to take a few cuts at the prewritten spots, all neatly handwritten on cue cards for their ease.

To tell you that we came out of there with Clio Award-caliber commercials would be as far-fetched as a no-hitter by Anthony Young. Even Yogi, later famed for his spontaneous palaver and magnificent assassination of rudimentary logic, sounded like a hearse driver on Valium. Finally, the last of the lot, right fielder Ron Swoboda, took some heroic stabs at the cue-carded copy. After several passable attempts, he paused and said, "Okay, I've got the basics down. Mind if I try it my way?" The cue cards were tossed and Swoboda began his improv, delivering an Oscar-worthy performance, especially placed alongside the "See Spot run" efforts of his immediate predecessors. Needless to say, NBC-TV chose to air the Swoboda spot 4 to 1 in rotation with the others.

One other gem from that day: Glancing at batting practice from the first-base coach's box, where we were wrapping up our taping, I watched as Tommie Agee lifted a lazy pop fly just off the first-base line, headed right for me. "Don't be a hero, get away. Let it drop!" yelled Yogi, who was tossing batting practice. Advice be damned, I was already backpedaling for my once-in-a-lifetime shot at a pop foul off the bat of a major-leaguer *on the field of play*. Somewhat disadvantaged—I was gloveless and dressed in a restrictive belted trench coat—I waited for the ball to drop from the sky. Dreams of the everyday fool stormed my brain. *This could lead to a tryout! I've got the eye of Gil Hodges's top assistant coach!* The moment of reckoning inevitably came to pass, and . . . yes! A bare-handed, bread-basket Willie Mays catch!

I should've kept the ball, for humiliation, swift and cutting, followed my highlight moment.

I one-hopped the ball back to Berra on the mound.

— A.R.

1

ORIGINS

They put fun into life. It was hell to play for them, but for anybody who watched them it was great. This was Bert Lahr in *The Wizard of Oz* or the Marx Brothers in *Room Service*. The Mets tried to play baseball, and the players trying to do it were serious. But the whole thing came out as great comedy, and it was the tonic the sport needed. People did not follow the Mets. They loved the Mets.

Jimmy Breslin

Pulitzer Prize-winning journalist/author

When the team was still in the planning stages, more than 2,500 letters arrived at Bill Shea's office, offering more than 500 different nickname suggestions. The top ten were: Continentals, Burros, Skyliners, Meadowlarks, Skyscrapers, Mets, Bees, Rebels, NYBs, Avengers, and Jets. The winner? Mets, with 32 votes. Second? Skyliners, with 31 votes.

Mollie Martin

author

FAST FACT: The Meadowlarks was Mets owner Mrs. Joan Whitney Payson's favorite choice.

They say we're going to get players out of a grab bag. From what I see, it's going to be a garbage bag.

Rogers Hornsby

*twenty-three-year Hall of Fame
second baseman/Mets super scout
in 1961,
on the 1962 expansion draft,
which supplied the Mets with their
first-ever player base*

One morning Casey Stengel was around his bank in Glendale (Calif.) and was telling everybody he was going to manage this new team in New York. "The Knickerbockers," he called them.

Jimmy Breslin

Her first name is Joan and she is a Whitney. She is of the world of the Social Register and charity drives and art museums and chauffeured Rolls-Royces. But this soft-talking 59-year-old dowager sat and talked of heavyweights and horses and nightclubs and first basemen. She could be the best person to come into baseball in our time. She knows more about how to lose with a laugh than anybody working for her except Mr. Stengel.

Jimmy Breslin

on original Mets owner
Joan Whitney Payson

Of course. How else in the world could we have gotten Marvelous Marv into New York? I think the whole thing was just wonderful.

Joan Whitney Payson

Mets principal owner (1962–75), asked if she would have spent her money on the Mets had she known how terrible they would be their first year (1962)

The first player ever drafted by the Mets was catcher Hobie Landrith, who had been in the league a dozen years without ever establishing himself as a starter. According to Casey Stengel, Landrith was the first pick because "you have to have a catcher, or you'll have a lot of passed balls."

Peter Golenbock

author

FAST FACT: Landrith played in just 23 games as a Met.

What did looks count against the kind of soaring hope that wrapped the Mets in silk and French perfume, as separate from reality as a lover's dream?

Leonard Shecter
longtime New York Post
sportswriter/author,
on the fledgling Mets,
spring training 1962

Stengel's boys took the field for the first time in earnest on April 11, 1962. . . . Gus Bell's second-inning single was the first Mets hit, while Gil Hodges's fourth-inning home run the first round-tripper. But the truer pattern was set in the final score: Cardinals 11, Mets 4.

Donald Honig
author/historian

From the start, the trouble with the Mets was the fact they were not too good at playing baseball. They lost an awful lot of games by one run, which is the mark of a bad team. They also lost innumerable games by fourteen runs or so. This is the mark of a terrible team. Actually, all the Mets did was lose. They lost at home and they lost away, they lost at night and they lost in the daytime. . . . The Mets of 1962, with 120 losses and only 40 wins, are the worst team in modern times.

Jimmy Breslin

They are without a doubt the worst team in the history of baseball. I speak with authority. I had the St. Louis Browns. I also speak with longing. I'd love to spend the rest of the summer around the team. If you couldn't have any fun with the Mets, you couldn't have any fun any place.

Bill Veeck

*owner of the horrific St. Louis
Browns clubs of the 1950s*

This was a new recognition that perfection is admirable but a trifle inhuman, that a stumbling kind of semi-success can be so much more warming.

Roger Angell

*writer/author,
on the Mets franchise's early
failings on the field before an
ever-growing and appreciative
public*

The first year of the New York Mets featured three 20-game losers, an Opening Day outfield that held the all-time major-league record for fathering children (19), a defensive catcher who couldn't catch, and an overall collection of strange players who performed strange feats. Yet it was absolutely wonderful. People loved it.

Jimmy Breslin

In their first year of play the Mets drew to the antiquated Polo Grounds 922,000 customers, in the process outdrawing Milwaukee, Chicago, and Philadelphia. They had proved something that was astonishing and perhaps unique in professional sports—losing does not necessarily have to be dismal or unprofitable.

Donald Honig

Things really disintegrated in '63. . . . We won more games, but we were bad.

Rod Kanehl

infielder/outfielder (1962–64)

Come see my amazin' Mets, which in some cases have played only semi-pro ball.

Casey Stengel

manager (1962–65)

Despite drastic cast changes and a promise of new scripts stressing drama of earnest conflict, the Mets still are enmeshed in the theater of the absurd.

Howard Taubman

The New York Times,
*on the Opening Day loss to the
Dodgers in 1965*

It was 1969 and Ed Kranepool, at 24, had seen more pathos on a baseball field in seven years than most men see in a lifetime.

Joseph Durso

author/longtime sportswriter,
The New York Times

I remember watching the '69 World Series on a black-and-white TV in the upstairs part of my house on the Jersey shore. I was five years old. I remember my father absolutely loving the Mets, because of Casey Stengel, and also my dad was of the underdog mentality. The Yankees were winning every year, and here come the lowly Mets, and he just fell in love with them. . . . We watched WOR-TV and listened to Lindsay Nelson and Bob Murphy on the radio. You didn't turn to WPIX (Yankees channel) unless you heard that Phil Rizzuto was saying some really goofy stuff.

Al Leiter
pitcher (1998–2004)

People used to laugh at the Mets. But not any more.

Ernie Banks

Chicago Cubs Hall of Fame shortstop/first baseman, on the 1969 Mets

Fifty-two days after man reached the moon, the Mets reached first place.

Joseph Durso

On September 10, 1969, the Mets beat the Montreal Expos, 3–2, in 12 innings to gain first place by half a game over the Chicago Cubs—the first time in the history of the franchise that the club had gained the top spot in the National League Eastern Division standings

This club plays better baseball now. Several of them look fairly alert.

Casey Stengel

on the '69 Mets

Seven hundred defeats later, here we are.

Ed Kranepool

first base/outfield (1962–79), upon taking the field for the start of the 1969 NLCS against Atlanta, the Mets' first-ever postseason appearance

2

THE BLUE
& ORANGE

From abysmal to amazin', from mediocre to miraculous, the Mets have marched through time under a canopy of evocative descriptions. Not all of them could be a Harrelson or a Hernandez, let alone a Doc or a Darryl. Some have been Marvelous while others were Terrific, but mostly it's been the day-to-day grinders that have brewed the Mets' magic, those whose shadows haven't cast quite as long as some of their better-known brethren. Others, like the new crop of Mets stars, simply haven't been with the club long enough to merit legend status. Here's to Mets moxie and those workaday mainstays who have helped build the foundation of the Blue & Orange.

That Frank Thomas is one helluva guy. But he makes a throw against the Cardinals. He's on third base and he makes a throw to first. He makes the wildest throw in baseball history. It goes 125 feet over the first baseman's head. Nobody ever done a thing like that. Well, what the hell, there never was a club like that.

Toots Shor

*legendary New York City
restaurateur,
on the former Pirates star who
came to the Mets in the 1962
expansion draft*

Be careful. He can tear your earbrows off. He's that strong.

Casey Stengel

on first baseman Gil Hodges

Richie Ashburn had a lot of enthusiasm for an old guy (Ashburn was 35). He seemed happy to be alive. Richie was an enthusiast and just lifted everybody's spirits.

Robert Lipsyte

longtime sportswriter,
The New York Times

FAST FACT: As inept as the original Mets of '62 were, they did produce an All-Star in Ashburn.

For years Jim Hickman was one of the Mets' best players. They didn't go anywhere until they got rid of him.

Leonard Shecter

on the New York outfielder from 1962 through 1966

Who is this brash fuck from Double A ball?

Richie Ashburn

outfielder (1962),
upon witnessing rookie utility infielder Rod Kanehl's aggressive challenge to veteran pitcher Roger Craig in a Mets' spring training session in 1962

He couldn't run. He couldn't field. He couldn't throw. . . . His failings were nothing less than spectacular. On a triple, he once forgot to touch first *and* second base. The press quickly dubbed him "Marvelous Marv," and he became a cult hero, a symbol for the marvelously inept Mets. Fans would chant his name and bring banners to the Polo Grounds celebrating his marvelousness.

Jon Scher
writer/author

Marv tried his best. But his best never quite cut the mustard, but rather left it splattered here and there.

Donald Honig

The hell of it all is, I'm really a good fielder.

Marv Throneberry
first base (1962–63)

Marv Throneberry can't snare a wild throw in the fourth inning of a July 8, 1962, loss to St. Louis at the Polo Grounds, one of three wild throws that passed the Mets' first baseman in the inning.

It wasn't easy to erase the memory of Lefty Bob Miller, the used-car salesman talked out of retirement by the Mets who made a spectacular comeback as a pitcher. His first pitch was slammed for a home run that cost the Mets a game and, two days later, his second pitch was slammed for a home run, costing the Mets another game. Lefty Bob's performance had that special tinge of Met lunacy: the first pitch hit over a fence in Milwaukee, the second hit over a fence in Cincinnati.

Joseph Durso

FAST FACT: Lefty Bob Miller, one of two Bob Millers on the Mets roster in 1962, toiled in 20 innings over 17 games for New York, logging an inauspicious 7.08 ERA.

Ed Kranepool had had a good high school career at James Monroe High School. I remember he came over to take batting practice with us for a look, and he hit balls out of the park. He hit the shit out of the ball. And everybody thought he was going to be a big home run hitter. I was in the on-deck circle when he got his first base hit. He came up, and he got a little slap hit into center field. And that's the way he hit. He was a slap hitter all the way.

Rod Kanehl

on the 18-year Mets first baseman/ outfielder, brought up at the end of the '62 season

Second baseman Ron Hunt put the bat on the ball and ran the bases intelligently. His trademarks—a chaw of tobacco in his cheek and a dirty uniform from a head-first slide—made him the kind of hard-nosed player Casey Stengel loved: cocky and fearless.

Peter Golenbock

I was the Mets' first All-Star voted on rather than designated. I played the game hard and I played it well, I thought. I gave it everything I had. I wasn't a contented player. I wanted to beat you any way I could.

Ron Hunt

*second base (1963–66)/
two-time NL All-Star with
New York*

Casey talked to me about getting hit. He said I would get 50 bucks or a suit of clothes. I didn't want the clothes. I didn't want to go to his tailor! I took the 50 bucks!

Ron Hunt

In his rookie season with the Mets, Ron Hunt batted .272 and was voted the team's most valuable player after leading the club in hitting, runs, base hits, and doubles. In the Rookie-of-the-Year vote conducted by the Baseball Writers Association of America at the conclusion of the season, the only player good enough to beat Hunt out for that award was a Cincinnati Reds rookie named Pete Rose.

Jack Lang
author/sportswriter

I thought he threw better than Johnny Bench. He could hold down a team's running game. He and Lou Brock had some classic battles. Talk to Seaver, Koosman, McGraw, talk to them. They will wave his flag. They will burnish his apple. And rightfully so.

Ron Swoboda
right field (1965–73),
on the throwing arm of catcher
Jerry Grote (1966–77)

If you looked up "red ass" in the dictionary, Jerry Grote's picture would be there. Jerry was the guy you wanted on your side, because he'd fight tooth and nail 'til death to win a ball game. If I had my career to do over again, Grote is the catcher I'd want behind the plate.

Jerry Koosman
pitcher (1967–78)

Jerry Grote was quick on the uptake. If a batter tried to peek back to see where he was setting up, he'd lean out from behind the plate and say to me, "If this son of a bitch looks back here one more time, hit him in the head." He was a tough player.

Jon Matlack
pitcher (1971–77)

If I was on the same team with him, I'd have to play third base.

Johnny Bench
Cincinnati Reds Hall of Fame catcher,
on standout defensive backstop Jerry Grote

He had more fun playing baseball than anybody I knew.

Ron Swoboda
on "Ya Gotta Believe" reliever Tug McGraw

Mister McGraw there, he's got the ear-marks of a splendid big-league pitcher. When he's got two-and-two on the batter, you might get a foul off him.

Casey Stengel

Gary Gentry was this western guy who just wasn't afraid of anything. He was a cowboy, a skinny kid with a tremendous arm. He was great. Gary demonstrated his fearlessness out on the mound where he made his living. Here was a kid, a rookie, who wasn't intimidated by anybody. He just let you have it.

Ron Swoboda

on the Mets' third pitcher in their 1969 rotation. Gentry went 13–12 on the season

Nolan Ryan was a wild high-ball pitcher in a low-ball league, which is like being a pair of brown socks in a room full of tuxedos.

Ron Swoboda

His style and grace on the field was eye-catching, earning him the nickname of "the Glider."

Maury Allen

longtime sportswriter/author, on third baseman Ed Charles (1967–69)

Getting Donn Clendenon meant a great deal. We finally had a legitimate home-run hitter. With one swing of the bat he could put us in the game or put us ahead.

Jerry Koosman

on the New York first baseman acquired from Montreal in 1969. In his three seasons with the Mets, Clendenon hit 45 home runs

Tug McGraw could pitch. Tug always had runners on base, always. Always let the shit get close to the fan. And the majority of the time he came out unscathed.

Ron Swoboda

Jon Matlack was a perfectionist in the way he worked out and the way he pitched. I can still picture his motion, bringing his arms up in front of him, just far enough that he could see through the vee in the bottom of his two hands. He didn't have an overpowering fastball— not as hard as Seaver and myself, but he was still in the 90s, and he had an excellent curveball and real good control. Jon was tough to hit.

Jerry Koosman

Craig Swan had the misfortune of having his best years during a period when the Mets were at their worst. He surprised everyone in 1978, when he led the National League with a 2.43 earned-run average, but his success didn't gain much attention because Mets attendance was at rock bottom and the press had pretty much stopped paying attention to anything the Mets did.

Peter Golenbock

Dave Kingman was moody. He loved to hit. He was strong. Jeez, he could hit home runs to left field with one hand. He could pull the outside pitch one-handed. But the guy couldn't hit an off-speed pitch. The only thing he could hit was a fastball.

Jerry Koosman

FAST FACT: Kingman hit 154 of his 442 career home runs in two stints with the Mets (1975–77, 1981–83).

Bobby Ojeda, a pitcher of quiet intensity, never really got the ink he deserved.

Peter Golenbock

FAST FACT: Ojeda, who pitched for the Mets from 1986 through 1990, went 18–5 in the world championship 1986 season, winning Game 2 of the NLCS—a 5–1 triumph over Houston—and Game 3 of the World Series, beating his former team, the Boston Red Sox, 7–1.

What really improved Bobby Ojeda when he came to the Mets was that he started throwing those inside fastballs, and he had a great change-up, probably the best change-up of anyone I ever caught.

Gary Carter
catcher (1985–89)

Jesse Orosco threw the way I always pictured that Satchel Paige must have thrown, with that whipping left arm that had so much movement on the ball. He was a loosy-goosy left-hander, so he was perfect for the job [of closer]. He didn't seem to think too much, and that was good.

Craig Swan
pitcher (1973–84),
on the Mets' reliable closer
(1979, 1981–87)

If I had to have someone in my foxhole, I'd want it to be Wally Backman. Pound for pound, Wally was as strong as anybody on our team.

Ron Gardenhire

shortstop (1981–85)/Minnesota Twins manager (2002–)

If Keith Hernandez was the heart and soul of the '86 Mets, then Wally Backman was the gristle.

Jon Scher

Roger McDowell and Jesse Orosco in the bull pen were as good a combination as there was.

Wally Backman

second base (1980–88), on New York's stellar relievers in the club's world championship year of 1986

When he returned to the mound, Roger McDowell found that his already outstanding sinker had mysteriously acquired the drop of the Coney Island Cyclone. It was a magical, career-altering discovery caused primarily by a slight decrease in arm angle.

Jeff Pearlman

*author/sportswriter,
on the dramatic change in
McDowell's pitches following
1984 surgery to remove bone
chips and spurs from his right
elbow*

He went to Yale. Shoot, the guy was intelligent, a good-looking guy who obviously endeared himself to New York. He had the perfect name. He was the darling of everybody. And once Ronnie learned to master the split-fingered fastball, he really matured as a pitcher.

Gary Carter

on Ron Darling (1983–91)

Here was a ballplayer that the average fan could root for and not worry about being let down. In his five previous years in New York, the center fielder's name never wound up on the police blotter, as too many of his teammates did. He was smart enough to know that people look at celebrities as targets. There was no evil in Mookie Wilson and no intentions, either.

Jeff Pearlman

Man, could he fly. I mean, as explosive as you'll ever witness.

Ed Lynch
pitcher (1980–86),
on teammate Mookie Wilson

He was a modern-day Frank Robinson: equal parts ass and god.

Jeff Pearlman

on first baseman Keith Hernandez

He's a gritty little player. What tees me off is he's only four-eleven.

Dave Parker

nineteen-year major-league outfielder with six teams, on Lenny Dykstra, the Mets' five-foot-ten fence-smashing center fielder (1985–1989), who once robbed Parker of a home run

If he was ever to settle for singles, Lenny Dykstra could hit .320, maybe even .330. It was the classic case of a midget wanting to be a giant. . . . Dykstra hit eight home runs in 1986. His goal was 500.

Jeff Pearlman

The Mets' surprise performer in 1987 was Terry Leach, the pocket side-armer who compiled a stunning 11–1 mark. Whenever Davey Johnson needed a reliever or was stuck for a spot starter, Leach got the call.

Jeff Pearlman

Sid Fernandez threw 95 percent fastballs, and he threw a curveball that no one ever swung at. It had a tight spin, he hid it so well that there were a lot of called strikes. It was the greatest thing in the world. He'd start it outside, and the batter would quit on it because they thought it was a rising fastball away, and it would stop and drop over.

Gary Carter
*on the Mets' southpaw ace
(1984–93)*

David Cone was a hell of a pitcher. Coney did his business on the field. You knew what you were getting when he went out there. He was a wild guy. He would have fit into the mix of players we had in '86.

Wally Backman

Fast Fact: David Cone (1987–92, 2003) was acquired from Kansas City prior to the 1987 season.

I'm the perfect New Yorker. I'm a hardass. I take no bull. I work hard, and I hate to lose. What more could you ask for?

Jeff Kent

second base (1992–96)

Fast Fact: Kent would blossom into one of the league's premier second-sackers with San Francisco and later with Houston and L.A., collaring the NL MVP award in 2000 as a Giant.

How could a 27-year-old pitcher with a live right arm lose a major-league-record 27 games in a row during the 1992 and '93 seasons?

Jon Scher

on the unbearable mound ordeal of Anthony Young, who went a combined 5–35 in his three seasons as a Mets hurler

It was a disaster, a nightmare for me and the Mets. But it's over with. I don't even want to look back.

Anthony Young

pitcher (1991–93), on his dubious 27-game losing streak

In 1996, Todd Hundley became a super-star, hitting 41 home runs to break Roy Campanella's record for most homers hit in a season by a catcher.

Jeff Pearlman

on the Mets' backstop from 1990 through '98

John Olerud has been a big hitter all his career. He's just a talented guy who goes unnoticed.

Bobby Valentine

manager (1996–2002), on the Mets' first baseman (1997–99), who hit 109 home runs during his previous eight seasons with Toronto and is the Mets' single-season record-holder for highest batting average (.354 in 1998)

Rickey is a Hall of Fame ballplayer. Absolutely, first ballot. I've played with a lot of great players, and he will go down as one I remember. I'll be able to say, "I played with Rickey Henderson."

Al Leiter

on baseball's all-time leading base stealer, a Met in 1999 and 2000

Turk's a good-hearted guy, but he's definitely a couple of cards short of a full deck. From his habit of eating licorice and brushing his teeth to having a tooth from every animal he's ever killed on a chain around his neck, he's definitely the wackiest guy I ever played with.

Al Leiter

on reliever Turk Wendell (1997–2001), who reportedly brushed his teeth between innings

If I were an everyday player, I would appreciate even more what Edgardo Alfonzo brings to the table, because everyday players view him as a really, really terrific ballplayer. He's a great hitter. You know he's going to give a good at-bat. He doesn't go into too many valleys and peaks. He's real steady. He's turned out to be a big force in our lineup and one of the better players in the league.

Al Leiter
on the Mets' infielder from 1995 through 2002

AP/Wide World Photo

Carlos Beltran

He's a true athlete. He looks like he could have run track or played football or basketball. I watch him and he just attacks the ball so fluidly. He's so gifted in a good way. I'm kind of like a lumber-jack. He's like a gazelle.

Mike Piazza
catcher (1998–2005),
on Carlos Beltran

He's a big-game guy. He's shown what he can do in the postseason. He has a beautiful swing. He's a very special individual. You don't see the ball jump off the bat like that with many hitters.

Willie Randolph
manager (2005–),
on Carlos Beltran, who hit .296
with three home runs in the 2006
NLCS against St. Louis

I certainly have been satisfied with his effort—110 percent. He's not satisfied with his performance, and he knows he can do better. He knows he will do better. He's a real pro. I mean, he was banged up pretty badly, and there was no way he wasn't going to play.

Fred Wilpon

owner (1980–),
on $119 million investment
Carlos Beltran's first season with
New York (2005), much of it
injury-plagued, during which the
newly signed free agent batted
.266, with just 16 home runs and
78 RBIs. Beltran rectified that
performance in 2006, however,
improving to .275, clouting 41
homers, and logging 116 RBIs

Beltran is my MVP, that's for sure.

Willie Randolph

August 2006

FAST FACT: In 2006, Beltran tied Todd Hundley's 1996 club mark of 41 home runs and earned his third straight National League All-Star selection.

Every time he pitches, it seems I have a good day. I wish he could pitch every other day, but I want to do well no matter who takes the mound.

Carlos Beltran

center field (2005–),
who began the 2005 season
with uncanny home run sup-
port whenever Pedro Martinez
pitched. Nine of Beltran's first 10
dingers came in games started by
the former Red Sox ace

David Wright emerged as a star in his first full major-league season and had the universal appeal and displayed the grit that suggested he would one day be named the team's captain. He was so popular, even 2002 Olympic gold-medal figure skater Sarah Hughes came to Shea Stadium for a specially arranged meeting.

Adam Rubin

New York Daily News *writer/ author,*
on the third baseman's sophomore 2005 season, in which he batted .306, with 27 homers and a club-high 102 RBIs

I have wanted to be a life-long Met and this is the first step in that direction

David Wright

third base (2004–),
on signing a six-year, $55 million contract extension in August 2006

David Wright

Hitting after him, I'm getting an inferiority complex.

Mike Piazza

*on left fielder Cliff Floyd's
hot bat in midsummer 2005 that
produced 20 home runs (34 on
the season)*

He's got the potential to be the best shortstop in the game.

Carlos Beltran

on Jose Reyes

The best feeling of all is sliding headfirst into third base with a triple.

Jose Reyes

shortstop (2003–)

The Mets are a good team, but when he's on base they're a different team. He takes them to another level.

Jim Tracy

*Pittsburgh Pirates manager,
on Jose Reyes*

Willie Randolph, not one for hyperbole, says Jose Reyes is faster than Willie Wilson, Bake McBride and Bo Jackson, and that he could be more complete than Derek Jeter.

Lindsay Berra
writer, ESPN the Magazine

Start with his signature statistical category. With 17 triples in 2005 and the same number in 2006, Reyes became the first major-leaguer with consecutive seasons of that many three-baggers since Paul Waner, Earle Combs, and Heinie Manush—Hall of Famers all—did it in 1927 and 1928.

Steve Hirdt
Elias Sports Bureau

AP/WIDE WORLD PHOTO

Jose Reyes

Jose Reyes can single-handedly shift the momentum of a game—with a gap-busting triple, or a ground ball beat out in a blue-and-orange blur; with a headlong, dust-churning dive when the gravitational pull of first isn't strong enough to overcome the draw of second, or a brilliant defensive play made possible by the quickest of feet and the strongest of arms.

Lindsay Berra

He has that fourth gear. And he gets from one to four real quick.

Dontrelle Willis
Florida Marlins pitcher,
on Reyes

He's my igniter.

Willie Randolph
on Reyes

When he goes, the rest of the team goes. He provides so much momentum.

David Wright

on Jose Reyes

> ***Fast Fact:*** The Mets shortstop slammed the club's eighth grand slam of the season—matching a franchise record, on August 6, 2006, three days after signing a $23.25 million, four-year extension. The blast, his 11th, also set a Mets season record for homers by a shortstop, breaking a tie with Kevin Elster (1989) and Ed Bressoud (1966). Reyes finished the year with 19 round-trippers.

Derek Jeter is terrific, but if he goes down, the Yankees can always plug in Alex Rodriguez at shortstop and go out and trade for Aramis Ramirez. Reyes is the Mets' resident irreplaceable part.

Jerry Crasnick

ESPN.com

That's Moses. He's all-knowing. Wisdom and knowledge, that's what he brings.

Paul Lo Duca
*catcher (2006–),
on the venerable Julio Franco*

If I only knew back then when I was young some of what I know now, I'd be looking at 3,000 hits.

Julio Franco
first base/pinch hitter (2006–)

FAST FACT: Franco, the "Speaker of the Clubhouse," turns 49 on April 23, 2007. He will be in his 23rd major-league season, though he has also played in Mexico, South Korea, and Japan for a total of 30 professional seasons.

He still has intimidation, whether hitters want to admit that or not.

John Smoltz
*Atlanta Braves pitcher,
on Pedro Martinez at age 35*

This guy is an unbelievable athlete. Duque can pitch for me any day. When he gets in a rhythm, he throws the breaking ball, the backdoor slider, working his spots, mixing his pitches, getting hitters off stride. He finesses you. He's smart. He's a pure competitor. I would love to have him back. I've always been one of his biggest fans.

Willie Randolph
on Orlando Hernandez

FAST FACT: Randolph got his wish. On November 14, 2006, Mets management re-signed the 41-year-old Hernandez to a two-year, $12 million deal.

I don't look at seven innings. I look at it one inning at a time, three outs. I get through that inning, I look at the next inning.

Orlando "el Duque" Hernandez
pitcher (2006–)

He's been a great citizen, a great pitcher. With a little break, he might have won 20 games. Everything we've asked, he has done it 120 percent. He's a man of his word, a man of character.

Fred Wilpon

*on mound ace Pedro Martinez
following the 2005 season,
his first as a Met*

He's had more 30-homer seasons than Mickey Mantle, more 100-RBI seasons than Reggie Jackson, and more seasons with both 30 and 100 than Ted Williams or Joe DiMaggio. But until 2006, when he was allowed to escape baseball's witness protection program, was there a more top-secret superstar in any sport than Carlos Delgado?

Jayson Stark

ESPN.com

Carlos Delgado was the perfect fit: a premier power hitter . . . and a charitable soul whom Omar Minaya calls "a better person than he is a player."

Tom Verducci

writer, Sports Illustrated

FAST FACT: Delgado blistered the 2006 playoffs, hitting .351, with four home runs and 11 RBIs in 10 postseason games.

He's one of those guys who always seems to bring teammates together from all different ethnic backgrounds. He's close friends with the American players. He's close friends with the Latin players. And this is a team with players from all over the world. It's Carlos Delgado who's kind of the big link who holds this team together.

Shawn Green

right field (2006–)

3

METS CHARACTER

I'm not one of those guys who is on the bench yelling, screaming. I'm very quiet. But when I have to say something I say it. . . . I know that some of the young guys look at me like a role model. I need to act like that. I need to play the game hard, do things right on the field and off the field.

Carlos Beltran

I hadn't been raised on the Mets legend; I wasn't part of that losing history. I never did find defeat particularly amusing.

Tom Seaver

pitcher (1967–77, 1983)

No matter who you are, no matter what you did, no matter what you accomplished, what happened last year is in the past.

Carlos Beltran

If you're going to play the game and you want to be a winner, you have to believe that you can.

Willie Randolph

You educate yourself. It was like Gil Hodges said to us, "Don't set low standards for yourself. It's not acceptable. You're a better team. It's unacceptable to throw games away."

Ron Swoboda

If you saw how Gary got ready for a game, how they taped him up every day, you knew he had to be hurt. He played with a lot of pain. He taped that knee every day and sometimes both knees. I don't know how many surgeries Gary ended up having, but I know he played more than half of his career in pain. That shows you what kind of an individual he was.

Wally Backman

on catcher Gary Carter's injury-plagued '85 campaign

Pressure is brought from within, and the way you avoid that is to just go out and play and hustle.

Gary Carter

There were periods when he was banged up and shouldn't have been in the lineup, but Ray Knight took cortisone shots and taped himself up, refusing to come out. Knight's gritty competitiveness provided a role model for the Mets' younger players.

Peter Golenbock

on New York's hard-playing third baseman from 1984 through '86

Ray Knight was a competitor. He didn't want to lose. As a kid he was a Golden Glove boxer. I used to watch Ray take cortisone shots in his hands just so he could play. Ray would do everything and anything it took.

Wally Backman

Ray Knight is unmatched in character. What he says is what he'll do. He's a true giant.

Gary Carter

He would have happily traded his spleen for a couple of victories.

Jeff Pearlman

on Wally Backman

They always say everything happens for a reason. The worst things you overcome can only make you stronger. I guess I hadn't figured it out yet, why the good Lord decided to just let my face be broken. If I look back on it, all I can say is, I got a chance to really experience something a little different.

Mike Cameron

right field (2004–05),
following his gruesome head-on
outfield collision with teammate
Carlos Beltran in a game against
San Diego, August 11, 2005, that
left him with multiple facial
fractures

Jesse Orosco was one of four players (with Tim Raines, Rickey Henderson, and Mike Morgan) to debut in the 1970s and last through the turn of the century. His secret? "A positive outlook," he says, "and good eating."

Jeff Pearlman

The outcome of this Series depends on your fortitude, your endurance, your perseverance, and your stout hearts.

Frank Cashen

*general manager (1980–90),
to his 1986 Mets prior to Game
6 of the World Series and New
York down three games to two to
Boston*

Immediacy of pleasure has ruined a lot of good baseball teams.

Rusty Staub

*outfield/first base
(1972–75, 1981–85)*

Mookie Wilson treated every day as if it were 75 degrees and sunny.

Jeff Pearlman

on the Mets' even-tempered center fielder of the eighties

If you look for what's wrong in people, you'll find it. My motto is to look for what's right in people. That's easier.

Mookie Wilson

center field (1980–89)

You have to be confident every at-bat. You can't be scared. You have to want to be there. You can't shy away from it.

David Wright

I've been in the game too long. I know all you need is one game, one performance, one outing—and you win a ballgame.

Willie Randolph

Take advantage when the situation arises. Know when you've got the upper hand.

Keith Hernandez
first base (1983–89)

🎾 🎾 🎾

There's a certain swagger. If you go out there and expect to win, other teams, it's almost like they fear you or they expect you to come in and beat them up during a series.

David Wright

🎾 🎾 🎾

You create your own momentum. You have to approach every game like it's the last game you're going to play.

Carlos Delgado
first base (2006–)

🎾 🎾 🎾

The more you overcome challenges, the more character you develop.

Willie Randolph

4

METS HUMOR

The first time we played the Yankees at the Stadium, we had a long rain delay. Robin Ventura dressed up in Mike Piazza's 31 uniform, put a fake mustache on, and ran around the bases in the rain. It was hilarious. Yankee broadcaster Mike Kay, talking during the rain delay, said, "I can't believe what an idiot Piazza is. He can get hurt. Why is he doing this?" Kay actually thought it was Mike goofing around. All the Yankees were laughing. We were saying, "George would never allow them to do that."

Al Leiter

It was our image that was toppled from its niche in the darkest recess of Cooperstown. It was from us that the Mets, with pitiful ease, wrested the titled of "The Worst Club in Baseball History."

Bill Veeck

on the 1962 Mets "overthrow" of the St. Louis Browns

The Mets is a very good thing. They give everybody a job. Just like the WPA.

Billy Loes

eleven-year major-league pitcher with Brooklyn, Baltimore, and San Francisco, on the '62 Mets

The Mets were in the field. Marvelous Marv was holding down first base. This was like saying Willie Sutton works at your bank.

Jimmy Breslin

The Mets achieved total incompetence in a single year, while the Browns worked industriously for almost a decade to gain equal proficiency. We employed Max Patkin and "Jackie" Price, both professional clowns. They beat us again. They had Marv Throneberry.

Bill Veeck

on the 1962 original Mets

Marvin Throneberry's teammates would have given him a cake for his birthday except they were afraid he would drop it.

Jimmy Breslin

They've shown me ways to lose I never knew existed.

Casey Stengel

on his 1962 Mets

I married George for richer or poorer, for better or for worse. But I didn't marry him for lunch.

Hazel Weiss

wife of Mets original general manager George Weiss, commenting on her husband's brief time of retirement, much of it spent at home, between stints as the Yankees' GM and Mets' GM

The fan that threw that back probably has a sore arm. It was so far up in the stands, there was probably a relay.

Felipe Alou

former San Francisco Giants manager, on David Wright's enormous late-August blast off Giants pitcher Kevin Correia, a 426-foot shot that landed a few rows from the back of AT&T Park's left field stands

I simply cannot stand 120 losses this year. We are going to cut those losses down. At least to 119.

Joan Whitney Payson

prognosticating on the Mets' upcoming second season, 1963

The trouble is, we are in a losing streak at the wrong time. If we was losing like this in the middle of the season, nobody would notice. But we are losing at the beginning of the season and this sets up the possibility of losing 162 games, which would probably be a new record, in the National League at least.

Casey Stengel

on the '62 Mets 0–9 start, still a club record for consecutive losses beginning a season

I have a son and I make him watch the Mets. I want him to know life. You watch the Mets, you think of being busted out with the guy from the Morris Plan calling you up every ten minutes. It's a history lesson. He'll understand the Depression when they teach it to him in school.

Toots Shor

FAST FACT: The Morris Plan helped provide consumer credit to the poor, beginning in 1910 and running through the 1920s.

I don't want to look like a seventies-style Burt Reynolds.

Mike Piazza

asked if he might keep his moustache upon arriving full-bearded to 2005 spring training and learning of new manager Willie Randolph's strict facial hair standards

This is the first time it's great to be a Met fan since Teddy Roosevelt was in the White House.

>**Steve Somers**
>
>*WFAN Radio host,
>on the 2005 wild-card race
>between the Mets, Marlins,
>Astros, and Phillies. His reference
>is to the old 1880s New York
>Metropolitans of the American
>Association. They in fact folded
>(1887) well before Roosevelt
>took office in 1901*

We'll finish in Chicago.

>**Casey Stengel**
>
>*asked by a reporter where he
>thought the Mets would finish
>in their inaugural 1962 season*

He's the perdotious quotient of the qualificatilus. He's the lower intestine.

Casey Stengel

when asked if third baseman Don Zimmer was the guts of the 1962 New York Mets

I was hitting .330 in early May. I went up to Casey in his office at the Polo Grounds, and I said, "I'm hitting .330, leading the team in hitting. How come I'm not playing regularly?" He asked me how much I was making. I said, "Eight thousand." He said, "You're not making enough money to be playing regular."

Rod Kanehl

I don't think we can catch the Dodgers— unless we play winter ball.

Casey Stengel

after two straight wins in early August 1963

He is quick on the base paths, but that is an attribute that's about as essential for catchers as neat handwriting.

Roger Angell

on Choo-Choo Coleman (1962–63, 1966)

⚾ ⚾ ⚾

They're mahogany and we're driftwood.

Casey Stengel

his comparison between the league-leading Los Angeles Dodgers and his last-place Mets, in 1963

⚾ ⚾ ⚾

You want to know how bad we were? They should have put a disclaimer on the tickets to the effect that, "Anything resembling major-league baseball is purely coincidental." Ed Kranepool used to tell me, "We used to celebrate rain-outs."

Ron Swoboda

Baseball is a lot like life. The line drives are caught, the squibblers go for base hits. It's an unfair game.

Rod Kanehl

Your first at-bat in the big leagues is like getting laid for the first time. You're never going to forget it.

Ron Swoboda

Boy, when they made him, they threw away the molding!

Wes Westrum

manager (1965–67)
known for his malapropisms

That was a real cliff-dweller, wasn't it?

Wes Westrum

another of his infamous
malapropisms

On the second day of the 1986 season, the Mets recorded a rap album, *Get Metsmerized*. Picture Vanilla Ice on crack, MC Hammer with half a tongue, and Kurtis Blow without one iota of rhythm. Now put them all together and subtract any remaining shred of harmony, flow, cadence, and talent. Oh yeah—make sure the lyrics don't exceed a second-grade reading level. That's *Get Metsmerized*.

Jeff Pearlman

You don't win a World Series drinking milk.

Doug Sisk
relief pitcher (1982–87)

Fighting is like sex. It doesn't make any difference whether you're on the bottom or the top.

Bud Harrelson
shortstop (1965–77),
on his altercation with
Cincinnati's Pete Rose in the
1973 NLCS

My wife wanted a big diamond.

Mookie Wilson

*on why his marriage took place
on a baseball field*

⚾ ⚾ ⚾

On "Thanks Rusty [Staub] Day," July 13, 1986, Roger McDowell purchased 20 electric-orange wigs for his teammates to wear in honor of Le Grand Orange. McDowell was a guy who, after giving up the winning run in a game that broke the Cubs' 13-game losing streak, reported the following afternoon with a paper bag over his head; who threw firecrackers into occupied bathroom stalls.

Jeff Pearlman

*on the Mets' creative clubhouse
prankster. Staub, if you hadn't
guess it, had flaming orange hair*

Ridiculously rich people who live in Manhattan root for the Yankees. When they hear about a coming "Subway Series," they scratch their heads and ask their doorman, "What's a subway?"

John Leo

essayist, U.S. News & World Report

The Mets are located in Queens, where real people predominate. Yankee fans don't even know where Queens is. Luckily, their chauffeurs do.

John Leo

Choo-Choo would give you the sign and then look down to see what it was.

Roger Craig

*pitcher (1962–63),
on the early-years Mets catcher
(1962–63, 1966)*

If we're not careful, we're going to wear out the saints rooting for the Mets.

Edna Stengel

*Casey's wife,
whose circle of friends, including manager Gil Hodges wife's
mother, had been praying to
St. Jude, the saint of hopeless
causes, and St. Anthony, among
others, for the Mets to succeed in
the 1969 World Series*

⚾ ⚾ ⚾

I don't know about that. But I think God has an apartment in New York.

Tom Seaver

*asked by a reporter covering the
1969 World Series if he thought
God was a Mets fan*

⚾ ⚾ ⚾

Sometimes you can observe a lot just by watching.

Yogi Berra

*coach (1965–71)/
manager (1972–75)*

The way we're going, it's hard to keep your feet on the ground. You feel inebriated, high. If they could package us, I don't think we'd be legal.

Ron Swoboda

on the late-charging Mets of '69

We got a hot water heater and a Porta-Potti for the mobile home. Now I've got it made.

Tug McGraw

pitcher (1965–67, 1969–74),
on how he spent his 1969
World Series check

Damn. Now I've got to face Dwight.

Hubie Brooks

third base/outfield (1980–84, 1991),
upon hearing he'd been traded to
Montreal after the 1984 season
and would now have to bat against
Doc Gooden

Old-Timer's games are like airplane landings. If you can walk away from them, they're successful.

Casey Stengel

Some people give their body to science. I gave my body to baseball.

Ron Hunt

owner of the major-league mark for most times hit by a pitch, 243, over his 12-year career (four with the Mets)

I have to trade him while he's hot.

Casey Stengel

on original Met Don Zimmer's first base hit, after going through a stretch in which he went 0-for–34. Zim played just 14 games with New York, recording a dismal four hits in 52 at-bats for a .077 batting average. He was traded to Cincinnati

The last time Ed Kranepool hit the ball to left field, Leo Durocher was a nice guy.

Leonard Shecter

on the Mets' left-handed-hitting first baseman

That's about a $20 cab fare.

Carlos Delgado

on teammate David Wright's estimated 445-foot home run in late May 2006 against the Yankees at Shea Stadium

I sure hope you're not late because you were out shopping for *that*.

Billy Wagner

*closer (2006–),
to Pedro Martinez, regarding a particularly outlandish outfit that the Mets' star hurler wore into the clubhouse after he reported late, supposedly from oversleeping*

The history of the New York Mets has been written best on bed sheets and banners: some clever, others loving or angry or stupid or even metaphysical, like the one displayed during the summer of 1971: Should reincarnation exist, this bed sheet would like the opportunity to return merely as a bed sheet.

William Leggett
writer, Sports Illustrated,
1972

To err is human, to forgive is a Mets fan

Polo Grounds banner
1962

Neil Allen, the ace reliever, keeps pictures of hitters who have slammed home runs off him during the season. Alongside each photo is a blank space with the words: "Who's next?"

Mollie Martin

I could have fun in a stalled elevator.

Tug McGraw

One time a bunch of the guys went out to Disneyland when we were in L.A., and that night we got beat real bad. So [manager] Wes Westrum announced that Disneyland was off limits. Get that: Mickey Mouse was off-limits because he made you too tired to play ball, but Joe's Bar was all right.

Tug McGraw

At least we kept him off the bases.

Charlie Manuel

*Philadelphia Phillies manager,
on speedy Jose Reyes, who
launched three home runs in a
game against Manuel's Phillies
on August 15, 2006*

⚾ ⚾ ⚾

When Pedro Martinez wasn't pitching—which, unfortunately for the 2006 Mets, was more often than they would have liked—he was doing something to make people smile, whether it was donning a pair of blue boxing gloves and sparring or running around with a Yoda mask and little else.

Bryan Hoch

MLB.com

⚾ ⚾ ⚾

The last miracle that I did was the 1969 Mets.

George Burns

*actor/comedian,
portraying God in the 1977 film*
Oh, God!

5

LEGENDS

I'd trade my past for his future.

Sandy Koufax
legendary Dodgers Hall of Fame hurler,
on youthful pitching sensation
Dwight Gooden in the mid-1980s

I learned a lot from Tommy, who was a consummate professional. Pitching is a science and an art, and Tommy was a master. There were so many different ways he was able to win. He talked about it, analyzed it, pushed himself regardless of the weather. He was one of those people come hell or high water who was going to be the best he could be.

Jon Matlack

on Tom Seaver

Tom Seaver was a student of the game and a student of pitching. He was a very smart guy. He could have done anything else.

Bing Devine

general manager (1966–67)

Tom Seaver

I watched him pitch a one-hitter against San Diego, an afternoon game where he struck out the last ten batters. I don't think there was a foul ball. And he didn't throw anything but fastballs. It was the most awesome display of sheer power and location pitching I've ever seen. The guy was just phenomenal.

Jon Matlack

on Tom Seaver

Nolan's biggest problem was that he was a high-ball pitcher in a low-ball league.

Ron Swoboda

on young fireballer Nolan Ryan, whose overall record in five years with the Mets, at the start of his 27-year major-league career, was 29–38

Jerry Koosman got a lot of the tough matchups. If you have a choice, why would you burn your number-one guy against the other team's number one? You want to give your number one a chance to win for you. Koosman was number two, and he got some of the tougher matchups.

Ron Swoboda

Jerry had a fastball, and he came off the side of the mound and got that fastball in on right-handers, and I mean he ate them up. He kind of cut it a little bit, too. It ran in on right-handers. Boy, you talk about eating them up! Jerry made a science out of it.

Ron Swoboda

You take Cleon Jones, which was a very timid player once, and the center fielder can throw for distance now. Out here he stood near the center-field fence and threw the ball to home plate 400-and-something feet, and they're both from Mobile besides.

Casey Stengel

on left fielder Cleon Jones and center fielder Tommie Agee

Tommie Agee would catch anything that was hit out there. He had an unorthodox running style. He was fast, though he'd go after the ball with a kind of wobble. But he always caught up with the ball.

Jerry Koosman

Cleon Jones

Tommie Agee, the Mets' hard-playing center fielder, led the world champions with 26 home runs in 1969.

Donald Honig

FAST FACT: Agee roamed center field at Shea from 1968 through '72.

He was just a big-game player. He had come from a winning sports background and he didn't like losing. He was a key man on that team. When he made those catches in the '69 World Series everybody got excited. Not me. I had seen him do that too many times in school.

Cleon Jones
outfielder (1963, 1965–75), on Tommie Agee

FAST FACT: Both Jones and Agee were high school teammates at Mobile (Ala.) Training High, an all-black vocational school, in the early 1960s.

If Tommie Agee was not the most important 1969 Met, none was more important.

Maury Allen

The Shea Hey Kid.

William Leggett
on Tommie Agee

Having Willie Mays as your center fielder/first baseman—talk about giving you a pump! To turn around and see him out there, he was like God, like having three extra players behind you.

Jerry Koosman

Many of the New York writers made him out as a load that we had to carry, but quite the contrary, he helped *us* carry the load, especially the last month and a half when we got hot and put it all together.

Tom Seaver

on Willie Mays's presence as a Met during the '73 pennant run

He was still our best player. I begged him not to retire. He said, "Koos, I'm tired."

Jerry Koosman

on Willie Mays's intention to quit after the '73 season

Rusty Staub is the only man to have played for four teams and collect 500 or more hits with each of them.

Michael Lichtenstein

author

Rusty Staub could hit at midnight in a coal mine.

Davey Johnson
manager (1984–90)

Long before his first professional game, Darryl Strawberry was branded "the black Ted Williams." Hugh Alexander, a scout for the Philadelphia Phillies, called him "the best prospect I've seen in the last thirty years."

Jeff Pearlman

Was I supposed to walk across the East River next? Actually that would have been easier than reading every day in the papers about the miracles I was expected to perform.

Darryl Strawberry
*outfielder (1983–90),
on being dubbed the club's
savior-to-be as a 21-year-old
rookie in May 1983*

Darryl Strawberry

AP/WIDE WORLD PHOTO

Darryl, you're my security blanket. If you play well, I'll be around. If you don't, I'll be gone.

Davey Johnson

to third-year budding star Darryl Strawberry at spring training in 1985

The press, and our noisy city, built him up as a potential Mays or DiMaggio, a kid of such breathtaking talent that he ought to hit 40 home runs and bat .300 as a matter of course. I've even heard it said that he had the talent to hit 50 home runs. The expectation was a heavy burden to carry.

Gary Carter

on Darryl Strawberry

We'd think, *What if this guy really turned it on? What kind of stats could he put together?* You'd think about it and say, "My God, this guy could have been phenomenal." Darryl Strawberry could have had the same type of career as Ken Griffey Jr. It's unfortunate, because all he did was take a Hall of Fame career and basically throw it away.

Gary Carter

FAST FACT: Though he hit 335 homers and drove in 1,000 runs, Strawberry's vast potential went largely unfulfilled due to a staggering series of personal and drug-related problems throughout his 17-year major-league career. He is one of only two players in baseball history to have played with all four current and former New York teams: the Mets, Dodgers, Giants, and Yankees.

I thought Darryl Strawberry had the most power that a person could be blessed with when I first saw him. If Darryl would have done a few things differently in his life, you'd see a guy who hit close to 600 home runs already.

Wally Backman

I checked around to make sure he was relatively clean. Hell, none of us know who the Saturday nighters are—but what you have to look for is someone who has a dependency, and I was convinced Keith didn't have a dependency. That's why we made the deal.

Frank Cashen

*on acquiring first baseman
Keith Hernandez from St. Louis
in June 1983 amidst rumors of
the former National League
co-MVP's drug use*

Keith was a general on the field. He didn't go to the mound just to go to the mound. He knew what to say to the pitchers. He went there with intention. Keith was one of the most intelligent players I ever played with. He knew the game and everything about it. They say the game is eighty percent mental, and Keith was mentally prepared for every situation, and not only for himself, but for the rest of the team.

Wally Backman

Wake him up at midnight, and he'll hit you a line drive.

Davey Johnson

on the steady play of Keith Hernandez

I was thinking, *Jeez, he has some poise.* He was firing bullets, his curve broke three feet, and every pitch was a strike or close to it. What control he had. I said to myself, *This kid is seventeen years old, and the catcher isn't jumping all over the place for the ball. Wow!*

Davey Johnson

on seeing prodigy Dwight Gooden at Kingsport in the Appalachian League in 1982

Dwight Gooden, a phenom as a rookie, was deified as a sophomore (1985), going 24–4 with a 1.53 ERA. At age 20 he became the youngest pitcher ever to win the Cy Young Award.

Jeff Pearlman

Every time he took the mound he had no-hit stuff. He threw 80 to 85 percent fastballs, and he threw what we called his "Lord Charles," the big curveball. He was so dominant that he could win games with just the fastball. That's how overpowering he was.

Gary Carter
on Dwight Gooden

Doc was awesome. That's the only word you could use for Dwight Gooden when he first came up. He was flat-out awesome. He overmatched quality major-league hitters.

Wally Backman

Dwight Gooden is simply the best pitcher in baseball.

Davey Johnson
1985

AP/WIDE WORLD PHOTO

Dwight Gooden

Gary Carter was our first hero [in '85], getting late-inning and tie-breaking hits that turned around the first five or so games. His enthusiasm and raw energy seemed to make things happen from right out of nowhere and infected the entire team with a spirit. It was fun to be on the Mets now.

Darryl Strawberry

They always called him "Camera Carter," because he wanted to be in front of the media, but in my opinion, if someone didn't like Gary, it was because of nothing but pure jealousy. I never, never, never heard Gary say a bad word about anyone.

Wally Backman

I played against Johnny Bench at the end of his career, and all the things people have said about him, you have to say the same about Gary Carter. Gary took a young pitching staff and was the boss out there. He called the pitches, talked to the pitchers, and continued to build their confidence. He took a young pitching staff and turned it into a championship a year later. That says a lot about Gary.

Wally Backman

It was like having a big ol' chair back there.

Terry Leach
*pitcher (1981–82, 1985–89),
on catcher Gary Carter*

Gary Carter is a special player, a Frank Robinson type. He plays hurt. His total energy is in competing and being better than the other guy. It's very refreshing to see a player making a total commitment, reveling in it, and enjoying it.

Davey Johnson

John Franco was called the "Godfather" for many reasons, starting with his Italian descent. John is the organizer. He makes it a point to get everybody together somewhere, somehow. He really is the clubhouse leader. He's vocal enough to speak up, and he has the respect of everyone.

Al Leiter

on the Mets' 14-year southpaw closer

You have to be The Man to have a Major League Baseball game stop for you for a five-minute tribute, and then have five or six curtain calls. That's when you know you've done something. That's when you know you're The Man in New York.

David Wright

*on the 2005 season finale
at Shea Stadium,
Mike Piazza's farewell as
a New York Met*

As Piazza goes, so we go offensively.

Al Leiter

Because of where I've come from in my career, I guess I've never taken myself too seriously. I've been able to laugh at myself.

Mike Piazza

*on his humble beginnings as
a 62nd-round draft pick of the
Los Angeles Dodgers in 1988*

AP/Wide World Photo

Mike Piazza

6

FIELD BOSSES

The truth is, you ain't as good a manager as you are when you're managing the Yankees, and you ain't as bad a manager as you are when you're losing a hundred games four years in a row with the Mets.

Ron Swoboda
on Casey Stengel

At 73, coming from a run of ten pennants and eight world championships in 12 years of managing the New York Yankees, Casey Stengel, in 1962, gave what must be the finest performance of his life. . . . He went through 120 losses with a smile, a try, and a few badly needed drinks. He tried to teach his players. They simply could not learn.

Jimmy Breslin

Makes a man think. You look up and down the bench and you have to say to yourself, "Can't anybody here play this game?"

Casey Stengel

who once professed that watching opponents circle around and around the bases made him dizzy

The newspaper sportswriters, as a rule fairly horrible at writing quotes even from a plain talker, went overboard on Casey's double-talk gag. In doing so, they succeeded in losing much of his humor.

Jimmy Breslin

He made the Mets lovable.

Jack Lang
on Casey Stengel

The one thing that happens when you hang out long enough with Stengel is you realize he makes absolute sense.

Robert Lipsyte

If only I knew what he was talking about.

Joan Whitney Payson
on Casey Stengel

The columnists who drifted in and out would get chunks of what sounded like gibberish repeated as Stengelese and then leave, but if you stayed there long enough, you got to know who the pronouns were about, and then you could follow the course of the conversation and you'd have very interesting stories about baseball, and great discussion of strategy and technique. I really thought he was a genius. I didn't think he was a blithering old man like a lot of people did. I really thought he had a lot to say.

Robert Lipsyte

on Casey Stengel

Casey took a lot of pressure off the players. When the writers were around and the cameras were on him, he put on an act for them. He would joke a lot and doubletalk, and he would talk baseball with them into the wee hours of the morning. He was entertaining them, giving them something to write about to divert their attention and camouflage the result of the game. But in the clubhouse he was right to the point. He was very witty, very sharp—for a man 75 years of age—and you knew exactly what he was saying if you were willing to think about it.

Ed Kranepool

He liked young kids who liked to play and hustle. If you got on Casey's shit list, man, you didn't get out. You may not have known why you were in there, but by God, you didn't get out of it.

Ron Hunt

He was a strange little man. He would say things like, "It makes sense in the daytime and it makes sense at night."

Ron Swoboda

on manager Wes Westrum

When Gil Hodges was running the ball club, you always felt that things were sane. Hodges was a man of few words—all of them effective.

Tug McGraw

Gil Hodges knits this club together with that great talent he has for letting you be a professional—which is what every Met has wanted to be since the Middle Ages in 1962 and which is what every Met finally approached in the Renaissance in 1969.

Tom Seaver

He just seemed to be totally in tune with what was going on, anticipating every possible thing that could happen in the game. He kept you in the game. Gil would be down at his end of the bench, and you'd be where you were, and at some point during the game he'd lean down and say, "Matlack, what's the count?"

Jon Matlack
on Gil Hodges

I respected the guy. He was a good baseball man, knew how to manage, made decisions quickly, always ahead of the game. Always.

Ron Swoboda
on Gil Hodges

The big change came when Gil Hodges died. He was a person on the field who really made some great decisions. And when he left, we didn't have that strength of person making those good decisions. It was more by committee.

Jerry Koosman

FAST FACT: Hodges died of a massive heart attack at the conclusion of spring training in 1972, coming off the golf course after a round with several Mets coaches.

The Berra legend was already a quarter of a century in the making, and it came with a full complement of malaprops and apocryphal stories. But those who knew him knew that much of the Yogi Berra legend was the product of newspapermen and that Yogi Berra, in his milieu, was a very keen student of the profession he had been practicing with remarkable success for so many years.

Donald Honig

on the Mets' manager (1972–75) and former New York Yankees manager and Hall of Fame catcher

Yogi is a very shrewd man, an excellent baseball man. Some people might laugh at the way he talks. We don't.

Bud Harrelson

I think the Mets will win the pennant with Yogi. He is a good strategist and an excellent judge of pitchers, and he does not panic.

Phil Linz

second base (1967–68), who played under Berra, when the ex-Hall of Fame catcher managed the Yanks. Linz's prediction about Yogi and the Mets, stated in 1972, came true the following year

Yogi was always a very positive person and easy going. It just took a lot to make Yogi mad. Yogi was a player's manager.

Jerry Koosman

Yogi was good people. Yogi was more of an even-keeled guy than anybody I've ever seen. He was the type of manager who said, "Here are the bats and balls, guys, here's the lineup. Go do your stuff."

Jon Matlack

Joe Torre came in as player/manager in 1977 and he was super. All the players loved him. Torre handled the players well. He used what he had. There are only so many things you can do during a ball game, and it seemed he did those things.

Craig Swan

He is the type of guy who will eat a quarter and spit up three dimes. And it's because he always prepares himself. He would always work with you. He was always available to talk baseball, to physically help you, and to visually help you. He is expert in having relationships with players.

Clint Hurdle
third base/catcher/outfield/
first base (1983, 1985, 1987),
on Davey Johnson

A player cannot perform at his best if he feels that what he does today is going to affect his role tomorrow.

Davey Johnson

Davey wanted to do things his way. He was a talented manager, and he had success doing things his way, and he didn't want that success affected by having someone else tell him what to do. I didn't see anything wrong with that. I'm sure the front office might not have appreciated some of the things he did, but Davey had to have the respect of the players, and that's what Davey got. And that's what made Davey successful. If he didn't have management's support, that wasn't good for him, and yet, he won. You can't get rid of a winner.

Wally Backman
on Johnson

As a player, Davey Johnson was baseball's Renaissance man, dedicated to becoming more than just a stereotypical jock. In no particular order Johnson earned a degree in mathematics from Trinity University in San Antonio; spent off-seasons working as an associate with Major Realty, one of the Southeast's largest brokerages; owned a motel (David Johnson's Second Sack in New Smyrna Beach, Florida), a 50-acre horse ranch, three shopping centers, and six apartment complexes; earned licenses as a pilot and a scuba diver; and edited an investment newsletter for five hundred major-leaguers.

Jeff Pearlman

My philosophy is K.I.S.S. Keep It Simple, Stupid.

Davey Johnson

Don't ever be so sensitive that you commit your total being to doing what's right for the organization, because it hurts you when you do what you think is right and get jumped for it.

Davey Johnson

Davey was a no-nonsense guy. He was a guy whose one rule was, "Don't embarrass the ball club or me." You give him everything you got. That was his style, to play to win. Do what it takes to win. Losing was never a part of it.

Wally Backman
on Davey Johnson

No one on earth is under greater scrutiny or has to put up with more criticism than a baseball manager.

Davey Johnson

The toughest part of my job is coming back to my office after the game and rethinking strategy after everyone has gone. One thing you have to avoid doing is saying to yourself, "What if I had kept so-and-so in?" It's wasted energy.

Davey Johnson

In this town if you make a mistake—and it may only be a mistake in the minds of the press—they can bury you in ten minutes and run you right out of Dodge City.

Davey Johnson

Without a strut it's hard to have the ruthlessness you need to win big. It drives you to the next level.

Davey Johnson

Johnson manages the team with the sanest direction and the zaniest players in baseball . . . a bottomless talent pool of reformed substance abusers, prima donnas, glory hounds, media darlings, braggarts, barroom brawlers, fatsos, and crybabies.

Thomas Boswell

writer, The Washington Post/
author,
on Davey Johnson and the
'86 Mets

I never want to be known as a manager who buries players. If you put a guy in a doghouse after just one bad outing, he may never get out of it. And, practically speaking, you may be forced to go back to that same guy.

Davey Johnson

Give me a chance and I'll show you how to get there.

Bobby Valentine

to his players upon taking the Mets' reins in late August 1996

He made everyone believe that everyone was important on this team, even the bench guys.

Carlos Baerga

second base (1996–98), on Bobby Valentine

He's kept everyone involved and everything positive. We have a great attitude and you have to give Bobby credit for that.

John Franco

relief pitcher (1990–2001, 2003–04), on Valentine

I heard amazing stories about him. John Robinson, the famous football coach at USC, said that Bobby Valentine was the next best running back since O. J. Simpson. Men praise the kind of athlete he was.

Al Leiter

*on Valentine's legendary status
as a schoolboy athlete*

FAST FACT: During his three-year high school career at Rippowam High School in Stamford, Conn., Valentine scored 53 touchdowns and was the only football player in the history of the state of Connecticut to be named a three-time All-American consecutively. But Valentine opted for baseball, signing with Los Angeles as the Dodgers' No. 1 pick (fifth overall) in the 1968 draft.

Bobby makes things easier for the players. He knows when he's needed and he becomes kind of a lightning rod. And maybe he doesn't even realize he's doing it. A few times when he does something, everyone will scratch their head and say, "What's he doing now?" Maybe he's smarter than you think, and he's doing it for a reason.

Al Leiter

on Valentine

The Mets manager was becoming Billy Martin without the booze. The headlines were his, whether he wanted them or not.

Jeff Pearlman

*on Bobby Valentine, who
frequently stirred up controversy
with his impromptu and often
not-quite-thought-out remarks*

Bobby is a little controversial and really could care less about what people think; he kind of does things that are untraditional and not the safe bet.

Al Leiter

on Valentine

I just wanted to come in here and change the culture and the mentality and the focus of this team, and get these guys playing hard for these fans every day. It's how you prepare yourself and feel about yourself. . . . It's really just building a winning mentality.

Willie Randolph

on taking over the Mets' field operations for the 2005 season

I expect to win every year. That's just me. I know that's not easy. And it's not like I'm making a bold prediction. I'm a winner. I'm about winning.

Willie Randolph

Willie's a lot more quiet than I thought. He's a very easygoing, very low-key person.

Pedro Martinez
pitcher (2005–)

It's important to know what it feels like to play in September.

Willie Randolph
on learning to win in a pressure-packed season's final weeks

7

MAJOR MOMENTS

Gigantic play. Huge play. Bizarre play.

Paul Lo Duca

*on Dodgers catcher Russell
Martin's belt off the right field wall
in the second-inning of Game 1 of
the 2006 NLDS that was converted
into a double play unparalleled in
postseason history, in which both
outs came at home plate just
seconds apart. The two Los Angeles
runners became back to back on
the base paths because the lead
runner held up, thinking the ball
might be caught by New York right
fielder Shawn Green*

On September 10, 1969, they made a baseball equivalent of Sir Edmund Hillary's conquest of Mt. Everest, gaining first place when they beat Montreal while the Cubs were losing.

Donald Honig

*on the Mets' first-ever ascent to
first place in the National League
Eastern Division*

The Mets really *are* amazing.

Henry Aaron

*Braves Hall of Famer,
following New York's triumph over
Atlanta in the 1969 playoffs to win
the National League
pennant*

We're here to prove there is no Santa Claus.

Brooks Robinson

*Orioles Hall of Fame third baseman,
prior to the start of the 1969
World Series against the Mets.
Yes, Brooks, there is a Santa Claus*

People said they hadn't seen a catch like that.

Peter Golenbock

on center fielder Tommie Agee's fourth-inning backhanded stab at Shea Stadium's left-center-field wall to rob Baltimore Orioles catcher Elrod Hendricks of an extra-base hit in Game 3 of the 1969 World Series. An hour later Agee made an equally sensational catch, diving head first and skidding on the ground near the warning track in right-center to kill Paul Blair's certain triple

Tommy made those catches with two outs and five runners on base. If he doesn't catch those balls, five runs score and they take a 2–1 lead in the Series.

Ron Swoboda

Ron Swoboda's catch of Brooks Robinson's line drive would make him one of the most renowned of World Series heroes.

Jerry Koosman

on the right fielder's legendary circus catch of Brooks Robinson's ninth-inning low line drive to right-center in Game 4 of the '69 World Series that kept the Orioles from taking the lead. The Mets won it in the bottom of the 10th, 2–1

We're not remembered for much, and if you're an average player and you do something memorable in the World Series, you do leave something, like when they discover dinosaur footprints.

Ron Swoboda

on his fabled catch in the '69 World Series

After the ball bounced, it came into our dugout. The ball came to me, and Gil told me to brush it against my shoe, and I did, and he came over and got the ball from me and took it out there and showed the umpire. "There is shoe polish on the ball."

Jerry Koosman

on the infamous shoe polish incident in Game 5 of the 1969 World Series

FAST FACT: Orioles pitcher Dave McNally was charged with hitting Mets batter Cleon Jones on the foot after New York manager Gil Hodges produced the ball with Jones's apparent shoe polish on it. Jones was awarded first base, and the next batter, Donn Clendenon, hit a home run to bring the Mets to within one run of Baltimore, at 3–2. New York would go on to win it, 5–3, and take their first World Series, four games to one.

I never saw anything like it.

Joe DiMaggio

immortal Yankees Hall of Famer,
on the '69 Mets as world champs

It was the greatest collective victory by any team in sports.

Tom Seaver

on the magical Mets of 1969

It was a colossal thing that they did. These young men showed that you can realize the most impossible dream of all.

Gil Hodges

manager (1968–71),
on his 1969 world champion
Mets

Some people still might not believe in us. But then, some people still think the world is flat.

Cleon Jones
on the 1969 world champions

Yogi kept telling everyone to be patient, that a hot streak was coming. Few took him seriously.

Peter Golenbock
on manager Yogi Berra's belief that things would turn around for his 1973 Mets. Lolling in last place, 11 games out of first in early July, and with rumors flying that Berra would soon be replaced, the New Yorkers went on a second-half roll to take the National League pennant

The game was highlighted by a scuffle at second base between Pete Rose and Bud Harrelson that ensued after Pete bowled Harrelson over while trying to break up a double play. Harrelson reacted angrily and the two men tangled. The brief swing-out aroused the ire of Mets fans and made Rose a target for Shea Stadium wrath for years later.

Donald Honig

on Game 3 of the 1973 NLCS against Cincinnati, won by New York, 9–2 , giving the Mets a 2–1 lead in the series, which they eventually won—three games to two—to advance to the World Series against Oakland

It was one of those marvelous moments in sport when a man does not merely rise to the occasion but soars above it. The ballpark rocked as Mays circled the bases. Every player on the New York bench was up to greet him.

William Leggett

on Willie Mays's first game as a New York Met, May 1972, in which the 41-year-old onetime Giants immortal belted the game-winning home run in a 5–4 victory over his former San Francisco teammates

When you come back to New York, it's like coming back to paradise.

Willie Mays

center field/first base (1972–73)

On July 22, 1986, the Mets ran out of position players in extra innings against the Cincinnati Reds. After the ejections of Ray Knight and Kevin Mitchell following a brawl, relievers Roger McDowell and Jesse Orosco finished the game by alternating pitching and manning the outfield, swapping positions depending on whether a lefty or righty batter was at the plate.

Adam Rubin

The last time I hit a home run to win a game in the bottom of the ninth I was playing Strat-O-Matic against my brother, where you roll the dice.

Lenny Dykstra

center field (1985–89),
on his walk-off, two-run, Game 3-winning clout to beat the Astros, 6–5, and put the Mets up two games to one in the 1986 NLCS

It was the biggest hit of my life, and I didn't even hit it.

Ed Hearn

catcher (1986),
on Lenny Dykstra's dramatic game-winning two-run home run to beat Houston, 6–5, in Game 3 of the 1986 NLCS

If we don't win Game 6, we face Scott in Game 7. If we face Scott in Game 7, we lose. I hate to say that, but it's true. We don't go to the World Series.

Ray Knight

third base (1984–86), on going against the 1986 Cy Young Award winner, Houston's unhittable Mike Scott, who had already beaten New York two games in the '86 NLCS. Scott possessed one of baseball's most devastating split-finger fastballs. Coupled with the delivery of his monster pitch were assertions that Scott also doctored the ball—a charge widely held but never substantiated—giving it even more of a diabolical drop

The nightmares are that you're gonna let the winning run score on a ground ball through your legs.

Bill Buckner

twenty-two-year major-leaguer and Boston Red Sox first baseman in 1986, prior to Game 1 of the '86 World Series

Relax, it's over. We've won.

Lenny Dykstra

to teammate Wally Backman, with New York trailing Boston 5–4 in the bottom of the 10th inning of the legendary Game 6 of the '86 World Series, down to its last out but with runners on first and third and Mookie Wilson at the plate. Dykstra's calm call in the dugout was prophetic: the Mets won the extraordinary game in dramatic fashion

Mookie's at-bat—one of the most famous in baseball history—was vintage Mookie Wilson. What happened next was compelled, created by Mookie's cleverness and speed—a hitless at-bat that had wizardry to it.

Gary Carter

on the wild pitch by Boston's Bob Stanley in the bottom of the 10th inning of Game 6 of the '86 World Series that enabled New York's Kevin Mitchell to score from third with the tying run and moved Ray Knight, at first base, into scoring position

Bill Buckner, who played 22 years in the big leagues, awkwardly bent for the ball and, with a look of horror, came up with air. The ball skipped past him, rolling down the right-field line. Ray Knight, running all the way, came around third and scored the winning run before anyone could retrieve the ball. Buckner was never forgiven by the Boston press or public for missing Mookie Wilson's ground ball.

Jeff Pearlman

on one of the most famous plays in baseball history that decided Game 6 of the 1986 World Series, an improbable 6–5 Mets victory to tie the Series at three games apiece

Buckner knew who was flying down the line, and he was thinking about fielding the ball and racing Mookie to the bag. He was distracted [by that], and the ball jumped his glove, and was gone. [Red Sox manager] John McNamara was criticized by Red Sox fans for letting Buckner play the 10th with that bum ankle. The ankle never affected his glove, but because of it, he may have been worrying about Mookie's well-known speed.

Gary Carter

on the infamous Buckner Boner that brought a cataclysmic ending to Game 6 of the '86 World Series

People ask me, what was my favorite, all-time Mets memory: It's seeing Ray Knight landing on home plate and the riot that followed.

Dwight Gooden
*pitcher (1984–94),
on the Mets' landmark
come-from-behind victory over
Boston in Game 6 of the 1986
World Series*

It was a great moment in baseball, and I'm not denying that. But I think everyone wants to be recognized for what they truly accomplished. And I do think that has overshadowed what my whole career was about. Buckner and myself, our careers should not be defined by that one moment.

Mookie Wilson

The excitement grew and grew. It felt inevitable, like counting down the minutes on New Year's Eve.

Gary Carter

after the Mets added two insurance runs in the bottom of the eighth for an 8–5 lead over Boston in Game 7 of the 1986 World Series. Jesse Orosco pitched a perfect ninth to close out the world championship for New York

That last out will last a lifetime in my memory bank: Jesse striking out Marty Barrett, flinging his glove into the air and dropping to his knees, his fists raised to the sky. It was the greatest moment of my career.

Dwight Gooden

on the Game 7 conclusion of the '86 World Series

It's so quiet in New York, you can almost hear Boston.

Vin Scully

World Series broadcaster, on the Shea Stadium crowd after Dave Henderson's solo home run in the top of the 10th put the Red Sox up, 4–3, in Game 6 of the 1986 World Series

It's so noisy at Shea, you can't hear the airplanes.

Vin Scully

after Ray Knight's seventh-inning home run in Game 7 of the 1986 World Series gave the Mets a 4–3 lead that they increased later in the inning to 6–3, before finally defeating Boston, 8–5, for their second world championship

They were dead. Dead.

Vinny Greco

*clubhouse employee,
on the shell-shocked Red Sox
after their Game 6 loss to New
York in the 1986 World Series.
Twice Boston had been one
strike away from winning the
Series and breaking the eternal
stranglehold of The Curse of the
Bambino*

We were like Popeye when he eats his spinach. He's getting his ass kicked, and he looks down and out. But he knows he's got his stash on the side. We knew that we had yet to eat our spinach.

Bob Ojeda

*pitcher (1986–90),
when Boston jumped to a quick
3–0 lead in Game 7 of the '86
Series. The Mets ultimately
prevailed, 8–5, to take the world
crown*

Robin Ventura sent a long drive into the right-field stands for what should have been a grand-slam home run. Shawon Dunston ran home with the winning run. Todd Pratt, thinking the ball had caromed off the wall, touched second, ran back toward first and embraced Ventura. When they hugged, Ventura was called out for passing Pratt. None of the other runners were allowed to score. The Mets had won 4–3. Pratt had cost Ventura his grand salami and three RBIs, but the wackiness of the scenario sent it into the history books as one of the great moments in Mets history.

Jeff Pearlman

*on the conclusion to the Mets'
15-inning Game 5 victory over
Atlanta in the 1999 NLCS*

Mike Piazza had hit a couple of home runs off Roger Clemens and had his number. Roger was going to establish himself early; he came high and tight. The difference between coming high and tight and hitting a guy in the head is the difference between releasing in front of your ear or one or two inches to the right of your ear. It was kind of cheesy, not a good thing, poor judgment on Roger's ability to throw the ball inside wild. . . . Even with all that said, I don't see Roger trying to hit Mike in the head.

Al Leiter

on Clemens's celebrated beaning of Piazza in the nightcap of the Mets-Yankees Shea Stadium-Yankee Stadium doubleheader in July 2000

What everyone wanted to know was, "Did Clemens throw the broken bat at Piazza on purpose?" Clemens denied doing so, and then made the cryptic statement, "I thought it was the ball."

Jeff Pearlman

on Piazza-Clemens II, during Game 2 of the 2000 World Series—their first encounter since the infamous beanball incident only three months earlier. In his first inning at-bat, Piazza swung at a Clemens pitch and splintered his bat, with the barrel end spinning out towards Clemens on the mound. A piqued Clemens retrieved the bat and appeared to throw it back in Piazza's direction, making his "I thought it was the ball" explanation an item of high comedy

I just wanted to put the ball in play. Smoltz was pitching a great ball game. He was locating balls, outside corner, inside corner, throwing splits. He drove me crazy. When I stroked that ball, I was the happiest man . . . Only God knows how much we needed it.

Carlos Beltran

on his game-winning eighth-inning home run off Atlanta Braves starter John Smoltz to give the Mets their first win of the 2005 season after losing their first five games. The 6–1 victory also gave newly acquired Pedro Martinez his first victory as a Met, a complete game two-hitter

That's going to be one of the catches of the year. Just pure instinct. Just a young boy doing what he does best—react.

Pedro Martinez

on third baseman sensation David Wright's over-the-shoulder, bare-handed circus catch in short left field off the bat of San Diego's Brian Giles in early August 2005

Are you kidding? That may be the best I've ever seen . . . Well, David Wright just guaranteed he will be seen on scoreboards around baseball for the next twenty years.

Ted Robinson

Fox Sports play-by-play announcer,
from his August 9, 2005, telecast of the Mets-Padres, on Wright's sparkling barehanded grab

I only wanted to see Mike Cameron move his limbs. To me, this was the Theismann-L. T. play from *Monday Night Football* all over again. TV is usually quite willing to exploit gruesome moments, and I didn't want to be a part of that . . . I had many fans thank me in person for asking for restraint.

Ted Robinson

during the August 11, 2005, Mets-Padres game, in which the grisly head-to-head crash of New York outfielders Carlos Beltran and Mike Cameron sent both players to the hospital with facial fractures and concussions

Half of my face is numb. Everything is numb. My right eye is filled with blood from one of the vessels in there that broke. The braces in my mouth are really tight, along with the screws in my mouth. I'm just trying to take care of myself, make progress. The worst has already happened, and it's only going to get better from here.

Mike Cameron

nine days after his horrific collision with center fielder Carlos Beltran in an August 2005 game against San Diego

He has the center field mentality. We're both center fielders. We just went for the ball. You don't think about it. You just go for the ball.

Carlos Beltran

on the Beltran-Cameron crash

FAST FACT: Mike Cameron, a natural center fielder, was moved to right field against his wishes to accommodate Beltran when the prized free agent signed with the Mets before the 2005 season.

Jose Reyes became the third player in the last 25 years to hit for the cycle in a game in which he led off the first inning with a home run.

Associated Press

Reyes's feat occurred in a 6–5 loss to Cincinnati, June 21, 2006

FAST FACT: The others to do it were Tony Phillips (1986, with Oakland) and Mark Grudzielanek (2005, Los Angeles Dodgers).

It was a total nightmare. I've never seen two grand slams in the same inning.

Dusty Baker

former Chicago Cubs manager, after the Mets scored 11 runs in the third inning of a 13–7 romp at Wrigley Field, July 16, 2006. In the Mets' club record-setting inning, Cliff Floyd and Carlos Beltran each walloped grand slams, while David Wright launched a two-runner homer

That's baseball. Some days you feel good, some days you feel not so good.

Carlos Beltran

after hitting his second grand slam home run in consecutive games, against Cincinnati, July 18, 2006. Beltran also added a run-scoring double in the ninth, following his seventh-inning bases-loaded swat. The Mets won, 8–3

I got a lot of practice last night.

David Wright

on becoming the 13th player in major-league All-Star Game history to homer in his first at-bat, during the 2006 game in Pittsburgh. Wright's joke about practice refers to the preceding night's Home Run Derby competition, in which he belted 16 HRs in the first-round, before losing to eventual winner Ryan Howard of Philadelphia

No player in the history of the major leagues ever had a season with as many runs, as many hits, as many homers, and as many steals as Jose Reyes produced in 2006.

Steve Hirdt

FAST FACT: Reyes registered 122 runs, 194 hits, 19 home runs, and 64 stolen bases in 2006.

Carlos Delgado pumped one of the most mammoth home runs ever witnessed at Shea Stadium, a 450-foot space shuttle that landed on top of the center-field camera hut.

Jayson Stark

on the New York first baseman's titanic clout in the fourth inning of Game 1 of the 2006 NLDS against Los Angeles. Delgado, who appeared in 1,171 regular-season games over 13 years—most of any active major-leaguer before appearing in a postseason game—went 4-for-5 at the plate in the Mets' 6–5 win

A beautifully pitched ballgame. Big-money pitcher.

Willie Randolph

on 290-career-win pitcher Tom Glavine, following Game 2 of the 2006 NLDS, in which the 40-year-old shut out Los Angeles over six innings, allowing just four hits, in New York's 4–1 win

Tommy was the key. He just quietly goes about his business and he's a real leader on our staff.

Willie Randolph

following Glavine's seven-inning, four-hit performance in New York's 2–0 Game 1 victory over St. Louis in the 2006 NLCS, extending his postseason scoreless innings steak to 13

Every time you do something in October it means a lot. Hitting the home run today of course brings memories.

Carlos Beltran

whose two-run, sixth-inning, 430-foot home run off Shea Stadium's giant scoreboard in right-center provided the Mets with all the runs they needed in their 2–0 win over St. Louis in Game 1 of the 2006 NLCS. The Cardinals had felt the brunt of Beltran before in October, when he batted .417 with four homers and five RBIs for the Astros in the 2004 NLCS, which St. Louis won in seven games

Maine had the poise of a Hall of Fame-type pitcher.

Shawn Green

*on the first-year Mets hurler
who won Game 6 of the 2006
NLCS, allowing St. Louis just two
first-inning hits before exiting in
the sixth with a 4–0 lead. In the
regular season, Maine worked
26 consecutive scoreless innings
from July 15 to August 12
en route to a 6–5 record and
3.60 ERA*

In Game 1 of the 2006 NLCS, Endy Chavez came off the bench to bring his unique blend of athleticism to the table, contributing one of the great catches of all time in Game 7 in robbing the Cardinals' Scott Rolen of a two-run homer.

Bryan Hoch

8

NEW YORK METS ALL-TIME TEAM

While Mets fans' fields of view are understand-ably maxed out with the magnificence of current stars David Wright, Jose Reyes, Carlos Beltran, and Carlos Delgado, it is mindful to note that none have been on the Mets roster more than four years, an all-time-team-killing stat. Consensus reigns at several positions—pitcher and right field, for instance—but arguments may abound at other points on the diamond, like at catcher, where three different All-Stars have excellently squatted behind the plate.

One egregious oversight remains inarguable: the hallowed doors of baseball's Valhalla in Cooperstown have opened to only one Met "lifer"—Tom Seaver.

KEITH HERNANDEZ
First base (1983–89)

Keith Hernandez was a very smart and very intense player, and when the game was on the line he was always able to keep his emotions from getting involved in the situations. I played fourteen seasons in the major leagues and Keith was the best clutch hitter I ever played with.

Wally Backman

He's the Baryshnikov of first basemen.

Tim McCarver

former St. Louis-Philadelphia catcher/broadcast analyst, on Keith Hernandez

RON HUNT
Second base (1963–66)

⚾ ⚾ ⚾

This kid has everything going for him, including an urge to cripple the opposition. When he tags anybody he leaves a black-and-blue mark.

Leonard Shecter

*on two-time All-Star
second baseman Ron Hunt*

⚾ ⚾ ⚾

When I got up to bat, I crowded the plate. I didn't give the inside or the outside of the plate away. And if I got hit, I got hit. I wore a blousy uniform anyway, and I just kind of learned to give with it. It didn't hurt quite as bad.

Ron Hunt

*whose 50 hit-by-pitch plate
appearances set a major-league
season record in 1971*

HOWARD JOHNSON
Third base (1985–93)

HoJo's got the best arm, the best speed, and the best power of any third baseman the Mets have ever had.

Bud Harrelson

In 1991 Howard Johnson became the second man, along with Bobby Bonds, to be a 30–30 man more than twice. Johnson swatted 38 home runs, stole 30 bases and knocked in 117 runs.

Michael Lichtenstein

FAST FACT: Johnson, in 1989, his best year with the Mets, hit 36 home runs and stole 41 bases, while batting in 101 runs and crossing the plate 104 times.

BUD HARRELSON
Shortstop (1965–77)

Buddy Harrelson at shortstop caught everything, and he knew the pitchers so well and how we pitched the hitters. If we did make a mistake, Buddy caught it, and if we didn't make a mistake, it was a can of corn. If it was a ground ball anywhere toward short, he was a vacuum cleaner out there.

Jerry Koosman

MIKE PIAZZA
Catcher (1998–2005)

🏐 🏐 🏐

He, in my opinion, is going to be the second Mets Hall of Famer. I think he loved being here and was certainly the star of the team. No matter who we had here, I think Mike was always the center point.

Fred Wilpon

🏐 🏐 🏐

Mike is one of those devastating guys in the lineup.

Al Leiter

CLEON JONES
Left field (1963, 1965–75)

⚾ ⚾ ⚾

One of the fine outfielders in Mets history, Cleon Jones's .340 batting average in 1969 is the highest ever by a Met.

Donald Honig

FAST FACT: Jones's mark stood for 29 years until broken by John Olerud with a .354 average in 1998.

⚾ ⚾ ⚾

When I was playing I could throw a football 60 yards in the air, and then run downfield and catch it.

Cleon Jones

an outstanding four-sport star in high school, along with fellow outfield mate Tommie Agee, in Mobile, Ala., before joining the Mets

MOOKIE WILSON
Center field (1980–89)

To see Mookie Wilson fly around the bases like Seattle Slew, a cloud of dust rising under his heels, was a glorious vision of athletic perfection.

Jeff Pearlman

Mookie Wilson's the perfect player. He'll do anything you want him to do. He never complains, and you never have to tell him to practice. Mookie is my catalyst. He's our speed on the bases, the guy who makes my offense go.

Davey Johnson

DARRYL STRAWBERRY
Right field (1983–90)

Darryl Strawberry was probably the finest all-around player ever to put on a Mets uniform. He could do each of the five basics required for greatness: hit, hit with power, run, throw, and field. The 21-year-old youngster, who followed Tom Seaver and Jon Matlack in becoming a Mets Rookie of the Year, batted .257 and hit 26 home runs in 1983.

Donald Honig

Strawberry was the graceful type of player who made everything look simple. The ball jumped off his bat like a firecracker. He ran like a deer. Keith Hernandez immediately compared the youngster to Willie McCovey, the Giants' future Hall of Famer.

Jeff Pearlman

TOM SEAVER
Pitcher (1967–77, 1983)

Seaver had Hall of Fame written on him when he walked into camp and pitched his first game in '67. He was a finished product when he came there. I don't ever recall the sense of him being a rookie. He came out of the box a big league pitcher, and there was this golden glow about him. This was clearly big talent, intelligent, capable, controlled, and awesome stuff.

Ron Swoboda

DAVEY JOHNSON
Manager (1984–90)

Davey was the kind of guy who let us go out and play. He didn't over manage, and it was one of his assets. He was the kind of guy who did nothing but put confidence into you. When Davey talked to us, he came out and said what he wanted to say, and he got through to you without screaming.

Ron Gardenhire

It's all for nothing if we don't win. Nobody is going to remember the second-place ball club. If you come in second, in memory you're no different than a club that finishes fifth. Close only counts in horseshoes and hand grenades.

Davey Johnson

New York Mets
All-Time Team

Keith Hernandez, *first base*

Ron Hunt, *second base*

Howard Johnson, *third base*

Bud Harrelson, *shortstop*

Mike Piazza, *catcher*

Cleon Jones, *left field*

Mookie Wilson, *center field*

Darryl Strawberry, *right field*

Tom Seaver, *pitcher*

Davey Johnson, *manager*

9

THE GREAT METS TEAMS

Like the Iron Chef, this is an offense that can carve you up 1,000 different ways. With flashing feet and top-to-bottom power. With patience and with brains. With the brightest faces of the 21st century (Jose Reyes and David Wright) and the ageless face of the dead-ball era (Julio Franco).

Jayson Stark

on the 2006 Mets

We never had a star on our ball club. We had a different star every day. Every day somebody was going to be a hero, and you didn't know who it was going to be.

Jerry Koosman
on the '69 world champion Mets

This here club doesn't make many mistakes now, you can see they believe in each other, and the coaches all live in New York and you can get them on the phone. I'm very proud of these fellows, which did such a splendid job, and if they can keep improving like this, they can keep going till Christmas.

Casey Stengel
on the '69 Amazin's

What happened was that a lot of good young players suddenly jelled and matured all at once. The chemistry on that ball club was a beautiful thing to feel and to see in action. Everybody had to contribute because we weren't that powerful, and everybody did contribute.

Tom Seaver

on the '69 world champions

People will never forget the '69 Mets. We caught New York by surprise; we caught the world by surprise. No matter where you go, people still want to talk about '69. Nothing ever replaced it. We won the pennant in '73, but people don't even mention it. They just want to talk about the '69 Mets.

Ed Kranepool

This Mets team was every bit as pugnacious, hard drinking, rough, and raucous as the old St. Louis Cardinals Gashouse Gang of the 1930s. That gang had some legendary fighters like Leo Durocher and Pepper Martin. This team had Ray Knight, a former Golden Glove boxer, and Darryl Strawberry, an L.A. ghetto kid who could turn mean when pushed too hard. Keith Hernandez could fight, too, and so could another of Davey Johnson's protégés, Wally Backman. This was a team that would squabble among themselves, but if pushed by the opposition would quickly start throwing punches.

Peter Golenbock
*on the Davey Johnson Mets
of the mid '80s*

A team on the march to the championship that develops this [fighter] attitude is no longer a team—it's more like a gang. You hang together, you chill together, you go to war together. You play kick-ass baseball until you're the only ones standing on the field. The machismo builds until you're no longer human, you're like a Terminator.

Darryl Strawberry

on the 1986 Mets

This was a team that, for all its night activities, possessed tremendous pride. There was still one thing more important than guzzling beer and meeting chicks: winning.

Jeff Pearlman

on the 1986 world champions

We were just a nasty bunch of guys. We'd go into a town and say, "We're gonna drink their beer, we're gonna beat their team, we're gonna kick their asses, and then we're gonna leave and do it to someone else."

Bob Ojeda
on the '86 Mets

Depending on whose brow is furrowed or whose nose is out of joint, this gang of toughs from the Big Apple is either arrogant, cocky, obnoxious, or, better yet, (D) all of the above.

Bob Verdi
The Sporting News,
on the '86 Mets

In 1986 the New York Mets spent every day under the giant-sized tent of the Big Apple Circus. Things moved at 10,000 mph—a hard-to-track swirl of baseball and booze and women and drugs and cars and fans and wins.

Jeff Pearlman

It was the best group I'd ever caught. I had some great individuals in Montreal, but never this type of quality, back to back to back to back. That's where the confidence of our club came from. With good pitching you can do everything. We had pitching. Nobody could touch us.

Gary Carter

*on the 1986 rotation of
Dwight Gooden, Ron Darling,
Bob Ojeda, and Sid Fernandez*

If you would've told me in spring training that we'd have a nine-and-a-half-game lead at this time of year, it would've been a good dream. You sleep a little better nine and a half games up. You give yourself a cushion.

Omar Minaya

general manager (2005–),
June 15, 2006

FAST FACT: New York would win the NL East by 12 games, ending Atlanta's unprecedented string of 14 consecutive division titles. During its early-season run, New York set a major-league record by winning eight consecutive games on the road when scoring in the first inning, breaking the 1939 Yankees' mark of seven straight games.

The architecture of these new Mets is a work in progress. The concrete is still wet.

Tom Verducci

on the 2006 NL East champions

When you play us, you see two of the most talented players in the league (Jose Reyes and Carlos Beltran) in the first inning.

Tom Glavine
pitcher (2003–),
on the 2006 New York Mets

We said from Day 1 that it won't be about individuals, it'll be about the team. That's how we play the game.

Omar Minaya
on the 2006 NLDS champions

We proved we can out-slug people, we can win with our legs, and we can play small ball. I think we're a complete team.

Paul Lo Duca
on the 2006 Mets

This team has a lot of confidence. We believe in ourselves. We just had a certain toughness as a team that carried us through a lot. We definitely got the most out of our group, the guys who were here.

Willie Randolph

on the '05 Mets

There are a lot of teams that are more talented than we are. But I don't think there's any team that plays harder than we do.

Willie Randolph

on the 2005 club

10

FIELDS OF PLAY

For Casey Stengel, there was probably a bit of nostalgia in nearly every ball yard in the country, but few offered the old boy as much sentiment as the venerable, peculiarly shaped place Stengel called "the Polar Grounds."

Donald Honig

on the Mets' home in 1962 and '63

I loved the Polo Grounds, loved the old ballparks. They were homey. Crosley Field, Wrigley, the one in Philadelphia (Connie Mack Stadium), even though the Philadelphia fans treated you badly. Even Forbes Field in Pittsburgh, as shitty as that old ballpark was, there was still something about it when you walked in. Maybe it was the idea of someone being here before.

Ron Hunt

It was a ballpark of an old and vanishing school, the Polo Grounds, wood rather than concrete, a fortune wasted in obstructed views, yet there was an unmatched intimacy with the game on the field for all of that.

Leonard Shecter

The Polo Grounds was a lovable freak. Its oval shape made it a polo grounds indeed, even if it was not conceived as such. It was only 257 feet down the right field line (they'll tell you Johnny Mize could spit that far) and 279 feet down the left, and center field was so far away only one man, Joe Adcock, had ever hit a ball into the seats out there. As a result, freak things had happened at the Polo Grounds.

Leonard Shecter

FAST FACT: In addition to Bobby Thomson's "Shot Heard 'Round the World" to win the 1951 pennant for the New York Giants, many "Chinese" home runs—lightly hit balls that just squeeze inside the foul poles or barely make it over the fence—were recorded at the vintage ballpark.

The charm of the Polo Grounds, as it was for all the old, angular, billboard-decorated baseball parks, was that its shape was a factor in baseball games. Given a one-run lead in the late innings, a pitcher had to try to avoid letting anybody pop the ball down the lines. Balls hit off the fence took funny bounces and only skilled outfielders played them well.

Leonard Shecter

on the original home of the Mets

It had been five years since a baseball was hit in anger at the Polo Grounds when the Mets got there. It was old and crumbling. Yet there was a style to the old place, and a feeling, a mixture of joy and despair—just the ingredients that made up the new team that had come to give the Polo Grounds its brief respite from inevitable doom.

Leonard Shecter
on the Mets 1962–63 home

At the end of '62, it was discovered that Shea Stadium was sinking into the bog, so we had to play in the Polo Grounds another year. At the end of '63, they did the same thing they did in '62: They presented Casey with home plate, and they played "Auld Lang Syne" as he walked all the way to our clubhouse in center field. And I cried again. I cried two years in a row.

Rod Kanehl

Lovely, just lovely. A lot lovelier than my team.

Casey Stengel

on first seeing the new Shea Stadium in 1964

Shea is a great big bowl, and when you filled it up, it resonated in a way that you can't describe. But when you are in this great big triple-decker horseshoe, the way the sound came out of there, it was a generator. Imagine being at home plate, which is the focal point of it all, or being in the field somewhere with the stadium vibrating. It literally vibrated. It was awesome.

Ron Swoboda

When you're young, it's great to go into a stadium where your future lies in front of you.

Casey Stengel
on Shea Stadium, 1964

The new ballpark, the first in New York City since Yankee Stadium opened in 1923, made Queens the fourth of five New York City boroughs to have a big-league club, following Manhattan (the Giants), the Bronx (the Yankees), and Brooklyn (the Dodgers).

Donald Honig
on Shea Stadium, 1964

To uppity New Yorkers, a visit to Shea Stadium was akin to sleeping in a sewer. The place (especially compared to palatial Yankee Stadium) was a housing project surrounding a diamond. Yet it was our housing project, and the Mets rolled out the red carpet for the average man.

Jeff Pearlman

You've heard of bat day and cap day? September 17, 1986, was Turf Day. Thousands of people went home with hunks of grass and sod. I wonder if they planted it in the backyards. Think of it: Shea Stadium grass sprouting all over New York, New Jersey, and Connecticut.

Gary Carter

on the fans' celebration that spilled over onto the playing surface at Shea Stadium when the Mets clinched the division title

This is what home-field advantage is all about. This place rocks. It's an imposing figure for a team that comes in here.

David Wright

during the 2006 postseason

The Flushing Meadow home of the New York Mets was and is an almost perfect ballpark. That bane of modern baseball—the artificial surface—does not deface this ballpark: in Shea Stadium baseball is played on real grass, as God and man intended it to be. The sight lines are unobstructed and equitable, allowing for neither immodest home runs nor extravagant fly outs.

Donald Honig

Chez Shea.

Lyle Spencer
MLB.com

11

RIVALRIES

From the time you were a kid, you always wanted to knock off No. 1. And they've been No. 1 for longer than most of us have been in the big leagues.

Paul Lo Duca

on toppling the incumbent Atlanta Braves, winner of 14 straight division titles, including 11 consecutive NL East crowns, on September 18, 2006

Oh, they were the enemy. Believe it or not, Whitey Herzog was my mentor. From day one he thrived at matchups. I learned that from him.

Davey Johnson

on the Cardinals rivalry

It was heated. I've been in some good rivalries. But we didn't like the Cardinals and it showed.

Ray Knight

Carlos Beltran has now hit seven homers in 11 National League Championship Series games, all of them against the Cardinals.

Barry M. Bloom

MLB.com

The Braves [had been] pretty much kicking the Mets' ass for a good period of time. New York, with its seven beat writers and all the media attention, begins calling them our nemesis and say the Braves are the team to beat, and the question is asked repeatedly, "How come you can't beat the Atlanta Braves?" It becomes a mental nuisance more than anything else, a snowball that continues to roll, and somehow, some way, you have to stop it. How you stop it is [to have] some lucky, good, miraculous baseball things happen that turn it around.

Al Leiter

You have to look at the reality of it, and the reality was that we didn't beat the Braves. They kind of had our number. So everyone tries to do their own little voodoo-type way to switch the luck, or change the formula to win, not think about it, think about it, don't talk about it.

Al Leiter

To be the team that ends a great dynasty is a thrill.

Omar Minaya

in 2006, after the Mets dethroned perennial NL East division champion Atlanta

The Cubs had an excellent ball club, just top notch. And whenever they would win, Ron Santo would jump in the air and click his heels, and it was an intimidating antic that he did for the opposition to see. Those kinds of things make you want to beat them worse; make you really try extra hard against them. Leo Durocher was a manager who tried to intimidate umpires, and it became a great rivalry. That was one club you loved to beat.

Jerry Koosman

I would have rather eaten shit than lost to the Red Sox.

Bob Ojeda
a Red Sox pitcher (1980–85)
before joining New York in '86

You know the importance of winning the intercity series. There's nothing like it. It's hard not to get amped-up for the Yankees. They're a measuring stick.

Tom Glavine

who notched his fifth straight victory of 2006 and 282nd of his career, in a 4–3 May 21 defeat of the Yankees.

One of the teams represents truth, justice, the American way, and underdogs everywhere. The other represents George Steinbrenner.

John Leo

on the Mets-Yankees rivalry

12

THE METS FAITHFUL

My involvement [as a Mets fan] was never as great as it was with Dwight Gooden. For Gooden, I created a new religion. I gave up Judaism entirely. I prayed to Good. I began to understand the concept that God is black. This guy was clearly black and he was clearly God.

David Brownstein

fan

The Mets gathered about them a breed of baseball fans who quite possibly will make you forget the characters who once made Brooklyn's Ebbets Field a part of this country's folklore. Mets fans are made of the same things. Brooklyn fans, observed sportswriter Garry Schumacher, never would have appreciated Joe DiMaggio on their club.

Jimmy Breslin

I've been a Mets fan all my life.

Popular phrase
sweeping New York during the hapless Mets' inaugural 1962 campaign

Any losing team I've ever been on had several things going on. One, the players gave up. Or they hated the manager. Or they had no team spirit. Or the fans turned into wolves. But there was none of this with the Mets. Nobody stopped trying. The manager was absolutely great, nobody grumbled about being with the club, and the fans we had, well, there haven't been fans like this in baseball history. So we lose 120 games and there isn't a gripe. Remarkable.

Richie Ashburn
after the 1962 season

The Mets are losers, just like nearly everybody else in life. This is a team for the cab driver who gets held up and the guy who loses out on a promotion because he didn't maneuver himself to lunch with the boss enough. It is the team for every guy who has to get out of bed in the morning and go to work for short money on a job he does not like. And it is the team for every woman who looks up ten years later and sees her husband eating dinner in a T-shirt and wonders how the hell she ever let this guy talk her into getting married.

Jimmy Breslin

A phenomenal thing was happening. With each loss the team seemed to draw more people around it. They were rooting for the Mets. And before the season ended, the team drew 922,000 into an old, poorly located ballpark.

Jimmy Breslin

on the original '62 Mets

You have to let the fans have fun. They come here to have fun and see the ball game. When you don't make a play, they're going to let you know you should have caught the ball.

Carlos Beltran

A lot of people identified with the Mets—underdog types, not losers—quality people who weren't quite getting it together.

Rod Kanehl

George Weiss and his assistant, Johnny Murphy, were akin to Richard Nixon and his Teutonic duo of John Ehrlichman and H. R. Haldeman, while Mets fans were more in tune with Yippie funsters Abbie Hoffman and Jerry Rubin.

Peter Golenbock

FAST FACT: Weiss, the Mets' first GM, tended toward a conservative, tight-fisted front office operation.

Our team finally caught up to our fans. Our fans were winners long ago.

M. Donald Grant

the Mets' first chairman of the board, following New York's clinching of the 1969 National League pennant

The attendance was robbed. We're still a fraud.

Casey Stengel

after the Mets' 7–0 season-opening loss to St. Louis in 1963

Mets fans came to Yankee Stadium with firecrackers and signs. Yankees fans had never seen this parading of signs and the throwing of firecrackers. We had to stop the game because someone had thrown a cherry bomb onto the field. It was great!

Rod Kanehl

on a 1963 exhibition game between New York's two teams

What the hell, so maybe I wasn't playing for the best team in the National League, but I sure was playing for the best fans in the National League. You owed them something. I never did forget the fans in New York.

Ron Hunt

What made the Mets truly different, truly special, was the depth of characters—foghorned Looie Kleppel and air-raid-siren-voiced Mother of the Mets, two fans who despised each other but loved the Mets from the far reaches of the Polo Grounds bleachers.

George Vecsey
writer/columnist,
The New York Times

They had brought so much goodwill, so much triumph, so many hours, weeks, and months of reflected glory for all the thousands who lived this dream vicariously. It was not simply a victory in baseball. It was for each observer an elevation of his own worth.

Maury Allen
on the miracle of the 1969 Mets

The Metophile is a dreamer. He believes that one day he will punch out that arrogant foreman at the plant square on his fat nose; that he will get in the last word with his wife; that he will win the Irish Sweepstakes; that the Mets will start a winning streak. The odds on the final possibility are somewhat higher than those on the first three.

Robert Lipsyte
1963

The fans here, if you need that little extra momentum, they will help you out. They will give it to you. It's fun to play in front of these fans.

John Maine
pitcher (2006–)

I never missed a Banner Day. I always sat in the dugout and watched the fans parade by. I thought, by God, if they could do something like that, I could pay them a little respect by sitting there and watching. Some of them were so clever. I was amused by it. Anyone who wasn't had to be dead or stupid.

Ron Hunt

The Mets were the biggest baby-sitting operation in the city. People would give the kids five bucks and send them to a ball game. And you didn't worry about them. They were going to be all right. The crowds in the summer when school was out were largely kids.

Ron Swoboda

A month after Woodstock, the Mets' seven-year famine was over. The fans flooded onto the field and grabbed anything that wasn't tied down, including hundreds of patches of sod. The infield looked like a World War I battlefield. Hundreds, maybe thousands, of others just sat on the outfield wall, dangling their feet and emoting a combination of joy and tears. They sat quietly and watched the scavengers strip the stadium bare of everything except first base, which was wedged too tightly into the ground to be moved.

Peter Golenbock

The New York Mets fans were good to me on the field, and they were good to my family off the field.

Ron Hunt

Montreal fans were good fans, but they really weren't baseball fans. They were more hockey fans. When I came to New York, it was a breath of fresh air. I could understand when they tell about meeting the needs of the New York fans, how they welcome you, how the fans can be your 10th man on the field.

Gary Carter

A few of the guys acknowledged the cheering fans and ran out on the field and started waving to the stands. The fans went crazy. More of us went out and began tipping our hats to our wonderful, wonderful New York Mets fans. The whole of Shea stadium was alive with love. It was warm. It was happy, it was like one giant 40,000-person family. . . . The fans loved us. We loved our Mets fans, loved them with all our hearts.

Darryl Strawberry

on the final regular-season game of the 1985 season, the day after the Mets, with 98 wins, had been eliminated from the playoff picture

The Mets were the product of the heart and soul of the people who swarmed off the ramp of the Number Seven elevated train, who sat on buses, who navigated ghastly traffic jams on the highways of New York, just to see a baseball team that made them feel.

George Vecsey

By the thousands, they gouged great holes in the turf, excavated home plate and the pitcher's mound, tore loose the bases. One man climbed the seven-story scoreboard, started back down again, then slipped and fell to the ground. In the first-aid room, the casualties streamed in like war victims.

Joseph Durso

following the Mets' clinching of the 1969 National League Eastern Division title

If there is one thing about a visiting player coming into New York playing against the Mets, for some reason they don't like coming to Shea. It's not the prettiest stadium, it's not got the best facilities, the clubhouse is old, and then you have to deal with the New York fan. As we know, he can be obnoxious. That all works to our favor.

Al Leiter

If the true meaning of "fan" is "a fanatic," that's what our fans are; they're fanatic about their baseball and certainly about their baseball team.

Tom Glavine

The chant of "Let's go Mets, let's go Mets" started early, about as soon as a small crowd of Shea faithful gathered near the home team's dugout. It continued and grew louder sporadically throughout the pregame workouts. And it reached thunderous levels when John Maine threw his first strike, recorded his first out, struck out his first batter and retired the side in order in the first inning.

Chris Girandola

MLB.com,
on the environment at Shea
Stadium prior to and during
Game 1 of the 2006 NLDS
against Los Angeles

13

THE
CLUBHOUSE

The final game of the 1969 World Series provoked such a frenzied outpouring of joy by Mets fans, including those in the Manhattan towers of finance, that thieves, seizing the confusion of the celebration, were able to remove $13.6 million in securities from the offices of Morgan Guaranty and Trust for what was then a world's record.

Gerald Astor
author/writer

Water is a blessing, so I got wet.

Pedro Martinez

*on his love of dashing through
on-field water sprinklers*

FAST FACT: On June 2, 2005, in the first inning against Arizona, the Shea Stadium infield sprinklers went off inadvertently. While umpires and players headed for cover, Martinez stayed out to play in them. Earlier, during spring training in Florida, he had raced through sprinklers with kids while filming a public service announcement for the Boys and Girls Clubs of America. On the final day of spring training in 2005, Martinez stood in the rain and sang "God Bless America." The man clearly must be a Pisces.

Mike Cameron's titanium plates in both cheeks and above his right eye caused him to set off an airport metal detector.

Adam Rubin

*referring to Cameron's
reconstructed face after the
devastating head-on crash with
Carlos Beltran in 2005*

I drink beer, I swear, but I wear my hair short. So I guess that makes me an All-American boy.

Tom Seaver

I didn't like playing exhibition games. I had a reason. I wasn't trying to snub the fans. I was programmed to get hit. When balls came inside, I didn't flinch from them, so when I was playing in an exhibition game, whether it was at Yankee Stadium or some minor-league park, I worried that a pitcher would come inside on me and break my wrist. For an exhibition game? Because I'm programmed not to get out of the way. I just get hit and think about it later.

Ron Hunt

Ya gotta believe.

Tug McGraw

*his legendary rallying cry to
teammates in midsummer 1973
that helped light a fire under the
last-place Mets, helping lift them
to the National League pennant*

FAST FACT: McGraw, down and dejected through
much of the first half of the 1973 season, was told by
a friend that he must regain his self-confidence, that
he had to begin believing in himself again. McGraw
ingested the advice and began his own locker room
campaign to boost fellow teammates. The phrase
became the club's focal point of inspiration, as the
Miracle Mets pulled themselves up, taking dead aim at
the NL flag. McGraw would lead by example: Over the
final five weeks of the season, the sparkplug southpaw
reliever made twenty mound appearances, allowing a
total of just four runs without blowing a single save.

I was criticized at times for being too accommodating to the press, but I felt it was part of the job. A lot of guys would duck into the trainer's room to avoid the press. I got the nickname "Camera Carter" and "Teeths" because I was always smiling. There was a lot of back-stabbing going on, and yet, the way you turn those things to the better, you hit them with kindness.

Gary Carter

We were a traveling rock show. When we were coming into town, everywhere we went would be packed with girls. Word always got around: "The Mets are here."

Ron Darling
pitcher (1983–91)

We took one in a row.

Mets fan

on the Mets' first win (9–1 over Pittsburgh) in their inaugural 1962 season, after opening with nine straight losses. New York then promptly resumed its defeatist ways, falling to Cincinnati in its 11th game

It's all about pitching, pitching, pitching.

Omar Minaya

If the Mets' first four starting pitchers were football players, they would be known as the Fearsome Foursome or the Purple People Eaters or the Steel Curtain.

Murray Chass

writer, The New York Times, *on the Gooden-Darling-Ojeda-Fernandez rotation of 1986 that combined for a 35–9 won-lost record and a 2.89 ERA through July 1*

In the 1986 All-Star Game Home Run Contest, Darryl Strawberry joined Mike Schmidt as the only men in history to ever hit one of the Astrodome's ceiling PA speakers.

Jeff Pearlman

Forget about Nolan Ryan for Jim Fregosi. The four-year, $12 million contract the Mets gave Vince Coleman in December 1990 will go down in history as the worst deal the club ever made.

Jon Scher

FAST FACT: The former St. Louis speedster was a disastrous acquisition by New York. Injured much of his first two years as a Met (1991–93), Coleman disappointed on the field and alienated teammates and fans alike with his antics off it.

Darryl Strawberry's first experience with cocaine came in 1983, shortly after he was promoted to the major leagues. While he had long been a beer drinker, it was not until his debut season that Strawberry came face-to-face with a powder that two decades later would leave him broke, imprisoned, and abandoned.

Jeff Pearlman

Tom Seaver believed mystically in the idea that he was the reincarnation of Christy Mathewson.

Maury Allen

Rusty Staub and Ty Cobb are the only major-leaguers to hit home runs as teenagers and after their 40th birthdays.

Michael Lichtenstein

It was a beautifully bizarre night. The center fielder [Lenny Dykstra] slid into the wall and almost knocked himself out. Between innings, on the big television screen in left center, they played a Three Stooges movie to amuse the crowd. Meanwhile, the cops were throwing somebody out of the stadium, and everybody stood on their seats to watch that. Then the PA announcer asked us all to stand and sing "Take Me out to the Ballgame" to welcome a contingent of visitors from India. Pure American Dada.

Philip Roth

author,
at Shea Stadium, July 25, 1985,
for the Astros-Mets game, a 6–3
New York victory

To ballplayers much of the writing about the game seems beside the point. On one end of the scale is all the junk, on the other is a vision of the game too romanticized or intellectualized, or both. Baseball is just baseball. We play the games. Winners and losers are designated. A lot of the stuff written about the "flawless symmetry" of baseball etc., etc., etc., falls on deaf ears with players, because it seems overblown, if not misguided. I keep the mysticism to a minimum. In my view of things, it has to be brought into the stadium by an outside agent; by a large white owl, say.

Keith Hernandez

Wow, Sandy! Cy Young!" I just thank God so much for having the opportunity to be mentioned with those names. I hope one of these days I'm mentioned with Roger Clemens or Nolan Ryan.

Pedro Martinez

after passing the immortal Cy Young for 16th place on the all-time strikeout list and Dodgers legend Koufax for fourth place on the all-time list for most 10-strikeout games

Crazy game. Sometimes you hit the ball hard and make an out. Other times you hit the ball soft and get a hit.

Jose Valentin

second base (2006–)

Eamus Metropoli.

Shea Stadium banner

Translation: "Let's Go Mets" in Latin

It was disappointing that we didn't get to the next level. When you get to the World Series, you're a part of history. Whether you win or lose, you're part of something very special. When someone says "The 2006 World Series," your name is going to be attached to that. And I just wanted my kids to be affiliated with that because of what we've done as a team, how far we've come in such a short period of time.

Willie Randolph
*following the Mets' 2006 NLCS
loss to St. Louis in seven games*

I'd make every year 1969 if I could.

Cleon Jones

14

METS WORLD CHAMPION ROSTERS

*T*he Mets' few but memorable trips to the Fall Classic, four in all, have produced two world championships, in 1969 and '86. Both times, the term "miracle" has dug its way into the descriptive lexicon of writers and historians covering those, well, miraculous times.

Here are the Series heroes—the Jerry Koosmans, Cleon Joneses, Ron Swobodas, Tommie Agees, Gary Carters, Mookie Wilsons, and the Ray Knights—plus New York's every day contributors, the "cogs," equally indispensable when it comes to hoisting a championship flag. The alltime New York Mets world championship rosters:

1969

107–63

(Includes 3–0 NLCS triumph over the Atlanta Braves and 4–1 win over the Baltimore Orioles in the World Series)

Gil Hodges, *manager*

Tommie Agee, *center field*

Ken Boswell, *second base*

Don Cardwell, *pitcher*

Ed Charles, *third base*

Donn Clendenon, *first base*

Jack DiLauro, *pitcher*

Duffy Dyer, *catcher*

Danny Frisella, *pitcher*

Wayne Garrett, *third base*

Rod Gaspar, *outfield*

Gary Gentry, *pitcher*

Jerry Grote, *catcher*

Bud Harrelson, *shortstop*

Jesse Hudson, *pitcher*

Starters in bold

Al Jackson, *pitcher*

Bob Johnson, *pitcher*

Cleon Jones, *left field*

Cal Koonce, *pitcher*

Jerry Koosman, *pitcher*

Ed Kranepool, *first base*

J. C. Martin, *catcher*

Jim McAndrew, *pitcher*

Tug McGraw, *pitcher*

Amos Otis, *outfield*

Bobby Pfeil, *third base*

Les Rohr, *pitcher*

Nolan Ryan, *pitcher*

Tom Seaver, *pitcher*

Art Shamsky, *outfield*

Ron Swoboda, *right field*

Ron Taylor, *pitcher*

Al Weis, *second base*

1986

116–59

(Includes 4–2 defeat of the Houston Astros in the NLCS and 4–3 World Series triumph over the Boston Red Sox)

Davey Johnson, *manager*

Rick Aguilera, *pitcher*

Rick Anderson, *pitcher*

Wally Backman, *second base*

Gary Carter, *catcher*

Ron Darling, *pitcher*

Lenny Dykstra, *center field*

Kevin Elster, *shortstop*

Sid Fernandez, *pitcher*

George Foster, *outfield*

Dwight Gooden, *pitcher*

Danny Heep, *outfield*

Keith Hernandez, *first base*

Howard Johnson, *third base*

Ray Knight, *third base*

Lee Mazzilli, *outfield*

Roger McDowell, *pitcher*

Kevin Mitchell, *outfield*

Bob Ojeda, *pitcher*

Jesse Orosco, *pitcher*

Rafael Santana, *shortstop*

Doug Sisk, *pitcher*

Darryl Strawberry, *right field*

Tim Teufel, *second base*

Mookie Wilson, *left field*

BIBLIOGRAPHY

Allen, Maury. *After the Miracle: The 1969 Mets Twenty Years Later.* New York: Franklin Watts, 1989.

Allen, Maury. *Baseball's 100: A Personal Ranking of the Best Players in Baseball History.* New York City: Galahad Books, 1981.

Allen, Maury. *The Incredible Mets.* New York: Paperback Library, 1969.

Astor, Gerald. *The Baseball Hall of Fame 50th Anniversary Book.* New York: Prentice Hall Press, 1988.

Berra, Lindsay. "Muy Rapido." *ESPN the Magazine.* 9 October 2006: 48-50, 53.

Boswell, Thomas. *How Life Imitates the World Series.* Garden City, N.Y.: Doubleday & Co., Inc., 1982.

Breslin, Jimmy. *Can't Anybody Here Play This Game?* Chicago: Ivan R. Dee, 2003 (originally published: New York: Viking, 1963).

Chieger, Bob. *Voices of Baseball: Quotations on the Summer Game.* New York: Atheneum, 1983.

Cohen, Stanley. *A Magic Summer: The '69 Mets.* San Diego, Calif.: Harcourt Brace Jovanovich, Publishers, 1988.

Devaney, John and Burt Goldblatt with Barbara Devaney. *The World Series: A Complete Pictorial History.* Chicago, Ill.: Rand McNally & Co., 1981.

Durso, Joseph. *Amazing: The Miracle of the Mets.* Boston, Mass.: Houghton Mifflin Co., 1970.

Dykstra, Lenny with Marty Noble. *Nails: The Inside Story of an Amazin' Season.* Garden City, N.Y.: Doubleday & Co., Inc., 1987.

Golenbock, Peter. *Amazin': The Miraculous History of New York's Most Beloved Baseball Team.* New York: St. Martin's Press, 2002.

Hernandez, Keith and Mike Bryan. *If At First: A Season with the Mets*. New York: McGraw-Hill Book Co., 1986.

Honig, Donald. *The New York Mets: The First Quarter Century—The Official 25th Anniversary Book*. New York: Crown Publishers, 1986.

Johnson, Davey and Peter Golenbock. *Bats*. New York: G. P. Putnam's Sons, 1986.

Kalinsky, George and Jon Scher. *The New York Mets: A Photographic History*. New York: Macmillan, 1995.

Lang, Jack and Peter Simon. *The New York Mets: Twenty-Five Years of Baseball Magic*. New York: Henry Holt and Co., 1986.

Leggett, William. "How Sweet It Is!" *Sports Illustrated*. 22 May 1972: 16, 18-19.

Lichtenstein, Michael. *Ya Gotta Believe!: The 40th Anniversary New York Mets Fan Book*. New York: St. Martin's Griffin, 2002.

Martin, Mollie. *New York Mets*. Creative Education, Inc., 1982.

McGraw, Tug and Joseph Durso. *Screwball*. Boston, Mass.: Houghton Mifflin Co., 1974.

Pearlman, Jeff. *The Bad Guys Won*. New York: HarperCollins Publishers, 2004.

Rubin, Adam. *Pedro, Carlos, and Omar: The Story of a Season in the Big Apple and the Pursuit of Baseball's Top Latino Stars*. Guilford, Conn.: The Lyons Press, 2006.

Shecter, Leonard. *Once Upon a Time…The Early Years of the New York Mets*. New York: The Dial Press, 1970.

Verducci, Tom. "Joy Ride." *Sports Illustrated*. 17 July 2006: 42, 44, 46-47.

Ward, Geoffrey C. and Ken Burns. *Baseball: An Illustrated History*. New York: Alfred A. Knopf, Inc., 1994.

WEB SITES

Associated Press. "Grand again: Beltran's 2nd Slam in two nights lifts Mets." http://sports.espn.go.com/mlb/recap?gameId=260718117, July 18, 2006.

Associated Press. "Glavine wins fifth straight as Mets take Subway Series." http://sports.espn.go.com/mlb/recap?gameId=260521121, May 21, 2006.

Associated Press. "Mets win 8th straight behind Wright's three-run homer." http://sports.espn.go.com/mlb/recap?gameId=260615122, June 15, 2006.

Associated Press. "Arroyo tosses CG, outduels el Duque as Reds top Mets." http://sports.espn.go.com/mlb/recap?gameId=260619121, June 19, 2006.

Bibliography

Associated Press. "Mets' Reyes hits for cycle in loss to Reds."
http://sports.espn.go.com/mlb/recap?gameId=260621121, June 21, 2006.

Associated Press. "el Duque dominates Bucs; Mets NL's first to 50 wins."
http://sports.espn.go.com/mlb/recap?gameId=260705121, July 5, 2006.

Associated Press. "Mets hit two slams in 11-run inning to quash Cubs."
http://sports.espn.go.com/mlb/recap?gameId=260716116, July 16, 2006.

Associated Press. "Mets snap four-game skid, beat Yankees behind Trachsel.
http://sports.espn.go.com/mlb/recap?gameId=260701110, July 1, 2006.

Associated Press. "Wright homers, Young's two-run triple in ninth lifts AL All-Stars."
http://sports.espn.go.com/mlb/recap?gameId=260711132, July 11, 2006.

Associated Press. "Mets sign Wright to six-year, $55M extension."
http://sports.espn.go.com/mlb/news/story?id=2541623, Aug. 6, 2006.

Associated Press. "Mets pick up first 3-game home sweep."
http://sports.espn.go.com/mlb/recap?gameId=260810121, Aug. 10, 2006.

Associated Press. "Beltran upstages Pujols-Delgado slam fest in Mets win."
http://sports.espn.go.com/mlb/recap?gameId=260822121, Aug. 22, 2006.

Associated Press. "Mets announce injured Pedro won't pitch in postseason."
http://sports.espn.go.com/mlb/news/story?id=2606427, Sept. 28, 2006.

Associated Press. "Glavine, Mets put Dodgers in 0-2 hole."
http://sports.espn.go.com/mlb/recap?gameId=261005121, Oct. 5, 2006.

Associated Press. "Green helps Mets break out broom on Dodgers in NLDS."
http://sports-ak.espn.go.com/mlb/recap?gameId=261007119, Oct. 7, 2006.

Associated Press. "Beltran's bat, Glavine's arm fuel Mets in NLCS opener."
http://sports.espn.go.com/mlb/recap?gameId=261012121, Oct. 12, 2006.

Associated Press. "Mr. Met: Maine's scoreless streak reaches 23 innings."
http://sports.espn.go.com/mlb/recap?gameId=260806121, Aug. 6, 2006.

Associated Press. "Offensive explosion helps Mets even NLCS 2-2."
http://sports.espn.go.com/mlb/recap?gameId=261015124, Oct. 15, 2005.

Associated Press. "Rookie Maine stymies Cards as Mets force Game 7."
http://sports.espn.go.com/mlb/recap?gameId=261018121, October 18, 2006.

Bloom, Barry M. "Carlos and Carlos clubbing Cards." MLB.com.
http://newyork.mets.mlb.com/NASApp/mlb/news/article.
jsp?ymd=20061016&content_id=1714502&vkey=news_nym&fext=.jsp&c_
id=nym, Oct. 15, 2006.

Blum, Ronald. "Mets clinch National League East title." Associated Press.
http://www.usatoday.com/sports/baseball/games/2006-09-18-marlins-mets-
clinch_x.htm, Sept. 18, 2006.

ESPN.com. "Jeter vs. Reyes: Who's more valuable?"
http://sports.espn.go.com/mlb/news/story?id=2603818, Sept. 27, 2006.

Girandola, Chris. "Shea alive, well...and loud for Game 1." MLB.com.
http://newyork.mets.mlb.com/NASApp/mlb/news/article.
jsp?ymd=20061004&content_id=1698978&/NASApp/mlb/news/article.

jsp?ymd=20061004&content_id=1698978&vkey=news_nym&fext=.jsp&c_id=nym, Oct. 4, 2006.

Hoch, Bryan. "Right mix made Mets winners." Special to MLB.com. http://newyork.mets.mlb.com/NASApp/mlb/news/article. jsp?ymd=20061023&content_id=1721543&vkey=news_nym&fext=.jsp&c_id=nym, Oct. 23, 2006.

Neel, Eric. "Hit-happy Mets pepper Dodgers into submission." ESPN.com. http://sports.espn.go.com/mlb/playoffs2006/columns/story?columnist=neel_eric&id=2617219, Oct. 7, 2006.

Noble, Marty. "Season-long effort pays off with title." MLB.com http://mlb.mlb.com/NASApp/mlb/news/article.jsp?ymd=20060915&content_id=1664939&vkey=news_mlb&fext=.jsp&c_id=mlb, Sept. 18, 2006.

Noble, Marty. "Resilient Mets rally to close out Dodgers." MLB.com. http://newyork.mets.mlb.com/NASApp/mlb/news/gameday_recap. jsp?ymd=20061007&content_id=1704098&vkey=recap&fext=.jsp&c_id=nym, Oct. 8, 2006.

Noble, Marty. "Randolph reflects on what-ifs of NLCS." MLB.com. http://newyork.mets.mlb.com/NASApp/mlb/news/article. jsp?ymd=20061023&content_id=1721893&vkey=news_nym&fext=.jsp&c_id=nym, Oct. 23, 2006.

O'Connell, Jack. "Friends of distinction: Mookie, Buckner." Special to MLB. com. http://newyork.mets.mlb.com/NASApp/mlb/news/article. jsp?ymd=20061025&content_id=1723459&vkey=news_nym&fext=.jsp&c_id=nym, Oct. 25, 2006.

Singer, Tom. "Randolph's optimism breeds gritty win." MLB.com. http://newyork.mets.mlb.com/NASApp/mlb/news/article_perspectives. jsp?ymd=20061004&content_id=1699684&vkey=perspectives&fext=.jsp, Oct. 4, 2006.

Singer, Tom. "Mets have overcome much to get here." MLB.com. http://newyork.mets.mlb.com/NASApp/mlb/news/article_perspectives. jsp?ymd=20061008&content_id=1705131&vkey=perspectives&fext=.jsp, Oct. 8, 2006.

Spencer, Lyle. "Maine pushes NLCS to the limit." MLB.com. http://newyork.mets.mlb.com/NASApp/mlb/news/gameday_recap. jsp?ymd=20061018&content_id=1717081&vkey=recap&fext=.jsp&c_id=nym, Oct. 18, 2006.

Stark, Jayson. "Some kind of blunderful for Dodgers." ESPN.com http://sports.espn.go.com/mlb/playoffs2006/columns/story?columnist=stark_jayson&id=2613645, Oct. 4, 2006.

Stark, Jayson. "Delgado making first October journey a memorable one." ESPN.com. http://sports.espn.go.com/mlb/playoffs2006/columns/story?columnist=stark_jayson&id=2627537, Oct. 15, 2006.

Street, Jim. "Mets hit 'em where they ain't." MLB.com.
http://newyork.mets.mlb.com/NASApp/mlb/news/article.
jsp?ymd=20061008&content_id=1705044&vkey=news_nym&fext=.jsp&c_
id=nym, Oct. 8, 2006.

INDEX

Index

Index

Index

Index

Printed in the USA
CPSIA information can be obtained
at www.ICGtesting.com
JSHW082157140824
68134JS00014B/286

9 781581 825787